W9-CLU-099

THE SMALL INVESTOR'S HANDBOOK FOR LONG-TERM SECURITY OR QUICK PROFIT

the text of this book is printed on 100% recycled paper

EVERYDAY HANDBOOKS

THE SMALL INVESTOR'S HANDBOOK

FOR LONG-TERM SECURITY OR QUICK PROFIT

REVISED EDITION

Ogden D. Scoville

BARNES & NOBLE BOOKS
A DIVISION OF HARPER & ROW, PUBLISHERS
New York, Evanston, San Francisco, London

This edition reprinted 1971 by Barnes & Noble, Publishers, through special arrangement with Sherbourne Press, Inc.

Library of Congress Catalog Card Number: 70-169526

ISBN 389 00336 0

Published in the United States of America

To my wife, Sandra,
Who makes it all worthwhile

CONTENTS

A BEGINNING NOTE

This is a practical book, written in everyday English, stripped of vague, high-sounding financial language (except when it is necessary to use a technical term which is explained immediately). It is a book you may use and profit from, now.

It is not a book for the college graduate in business administration, professional investor, or financial genius. Nor is it for the high-rolling, take-a-chance plunger, although there are pointers for the daring who wish to use high leverage techniques for speculating. It is meant for the men and women who would like to make their money work for them as hard as they worked to get their money.

This book is written so that you, the reader, will have a practical way to judge your future money needs and to prepare for your future emotional and physical necessities, luxuries, and dreams. It will enable you to choose an investment which suits your present-day needs and to formulate an intelligent program which will solve tomorrow's problems. It will show you practical ways to accumulate wealth.

The motto of my securities company is "We want to be your best financial friend." I hope this book will be that kind of friend to you and help your fondest dreams come true. It is intended to be a practical guide in making profitable investment decisions.

Good luck is mainly good information, promptly and wisely acted upon. So . . . good and profitable reading.

—OGDEN D. SCOVILLE
Glendale, Calif.

1

WHY INVEST?

Since the industrialization of the United States, we have made more technological progress than in any other time, culture, or nation. America has showered upon this world new knowledge, materials, products and production methods in ever-increasing amounts, and continues to do so. Americans are the world's production geniuses; our form of capitalism has provided our citizens with more luxuries than any other people. In fact, things that are luxuries in most of the world are considered bare necessities in the United States. There is a continual inflow of educated people from other nations (the brain drain), people who want to create and work so they may share in our abundance. The progressive ideas of American management have created more jobs, at higher pay and with less manual labor and physical danger. We have more homes, autos, and other material wealth, and America's technological lead in most fields of industry and science enables us to be very optimistic about our personal and national future.

A WORLD MADE BY TECHNOLOGY

Our world is becoming more and more the world of science. Almost half of the things we use and the machines used to make them were not in existence 10 years ago. Electronic marvels such as computers have taken us to the moon. We are seeing astonishing efforts in the relatively new fields of aerospace, bionics, modern communications, high-energy physics, miniaturization, and oceanography. New industries use exotic metal forming, nuclear isotopes, and radiation to create entirely new products and services. Investment in these industries and their suppliers will take courage, knowledge, and willingness to assume high risks. The reward could be extraordinarily high profits.

Continued change is guaranteed by the problem of developing new resources. In 1967 a commission was appointed by the President of the United States to study natural resource needs. They issued a report which stated, in part: "Consumption of metals in the next 35 years is expected to exceed that of the last 2,000 years. Energy use in the next 20 years is estimated at 3 times that of the last 100 years. World food production must increase by 50 percent over the next 20 years to keep pace with growing populations. We have enough water, enough resources to last us to the year 2000." We must face the fact that our world, as we know it, must change to meet the coming demands or it will not survive.

Technological progress means that in 5 years today's technology will be as out of date as the new car you just bought. The need for highly trained minds is apparent, for this means international leadership and economic survival. Today's college graduates in science have more knowledge than those of us who graduated in the same fields 20 or 30 years ago, despite our years of working experience. The physical and financial assets of today's corporations are not half as important as trained management that is capable of living with and adapting to our changing technological world.

Investment capital, using modern technology, can solve the world's material problems to the benefit of all.

THE MEANING OF INFLATION

What is inflation? It's a two-bit word that means the things you buy cost you more. It is a sneak thief that creeps along by night and day to rob you of your stored-up labor (money). It is the rise in the cost of living, and the Bureau of Labor puts out a monthly statement that usually says the cost of living rose by such-and-such a percentage this month to an all-time high. It is a $5,500 Ford...a 15¢ coke...a 15¢ candy bar that is half size; it's a 2-buck movie and a 50¢ loaf of bread.

It's what has been estimated will become a $700 a day hospital bed, a $4.40 pack of cigarettes, and a $3.30 loaf of bread by the year 2000, just 25 years from now and in our own lifetime.

Really, inflation has been with people since the beginning of time. You have seen the charts that say a 1900 dollar now buys 19¢ worth of goods, and you may ask who causes inflation. And the answer is simple. It's you, not someone else. It's you, the union man who demands a wage raise higher than the increased amount of work he puts out. It is you, the manufacturer who adds on more profit than his increased costs. It's also the manufacturer who bids up prices by acceding to high wage demands or higher raw material costs in the fear that if he doesn't get his share his competitor will beat him to it. And especially it is the lazy, the taker who produces nothing but added costs for the prudent person who works and invests.

It's Big Brother in Washington who wants to take care of all of us from the cradle to the grave, and Little Brother from City Hall to State Capital who builds marble tombs filled with paper-shufflers who love to tax and spend for our collective good.

It's you and me and everyone else who wants just a little bit more and creates the demand that drives up prices. When goods and services are in short supply, then it is our nature to pay that little extra cost so we may have what we want.

Think about first class mail and the postage stamp needed to pay it. You see it every day, and at this writing it says 10¢ postage. In 1919 the rate was raised from 1¢ to 2¢; then to 3¢ in 1932 (an interval of 13 years); to 4¢ in 1959 (17 years); four years later up to 5¢; the 6¢ rate came in 1968, and in 1971 it was raised to 8 cents. This tax has gone up 100 percent in 10 years. At this accelerated rate we could be paying 66¢ per letter by the year 2000 if postage rates keep up with anticipated inflation, and more if it outruns inflation.

We must realize that waste of either money or labor causes increased costs. Inflation can be held down to acceptable levels if all of us demand less from our governments and are willing to do more for ourselves. We must remember that governments do not create wealth but spend what is taken by taxation from everyone who earns. Since World War II, we have given away over $160 billion to foreign governments. In our national budget we have an expense of at least $9 billion for interest on this great giveaway which we will have to pay in taxes. At the end of World War II, Germany was a divided, beaten nation whose industries were destroyed and whose cities were in ruins. American cigarettes were used as money. American government experts advised the Germans to go into debt, and to tax and spend as the means to economic recovery. Ignoring this advice, the Germans adopted a plan that called for them to work hard, save, invest, and live within a reasonable budget. The mark today is a stable currency, and to many Europeans more stable than the American dollar.

Now let's describe a typical demand-supply inflation cycle. It starts when consumers want more goods and services than are available. Merchants and manufacturers find they can raise prices because of the demand by eager buyers, and there is very little resistance to these increased prices. In the business rush, labor is able to demand and get higher wages that are out of proportion to the amount of extra production. High employment means a shortage of skilled workers and the hiring of extra employees to hoard skilled labor. This cycle repeats itself and feeds back higher production costs. Since everyone concerned believes that he is only trying to keep up with inflation, preserve his markets, and get only his fair share, the inflation balloon keeps on rising. When goods price themselves out of the market, there are manufacturing cutbacks, unemployment rises, and supply exceeds demand. Then we spiral down to depression and bust.

WHAT INFLATION HAS ALREADY DONE

Let's look at specific groups of people and see how inflation has treated them over the past 5 years. I am using this 5-year period because it has seen high inflation and because people's memories are very short. History does repeat itself, but most people feel that anything beyond 5 years ago is ancient history.

Those who have benefited include factory workers who are in strong unions or have skilled jobs. There is a shortage of skilled craftsmen, and they have shown a net gain in their incomes of 6.1 percent beyond inflation. Home owners have been especially well treated. A house in most areas has gone up 38 percent since 1969. Since mortgage payments remain the same, these payments now take a smaller percentage of their income. Most incomes have risen also, and the rise in home value has been profitable. If you wish to move, though, you will find a joker! Your new house will cost you 38 percent more, and higher interest rates will make mortgage payments take a larger percentage of your current income than they did when you bought your 1969 house.

Social Security recipients have had a net gain of more than 7 percent, since their benefits have been raised every 2 years by Congress. Retired federal government pensioners have stayed ahead by 3 percent. Veterans' pensions have increased 12 percent more than inflation.

Businessmen have generally benefited, as they have been able to adjust their prices upward. Additionally, sales volumes keep on rising and there is more money in circulation.

The United States government has found inflation beneficial because income tax revenues rise faster and faster, due to the progressive nature of the tax. Bonds, notes, and other government debts are being paid off with cheaper dollars.

Common stock buyers have been both helped and hurt. It depends upon the stocks they own. The Dow Jones stock averages show that common stocks have not kept up, while the Standard and Poor index shows that they have kept up with inflation.

The investors who have taken losses include people who have kept cash or had large checking accounts. They lost about 38 percent, the same amount which was lost by life insurance policy cash values. The face value of life insurance also fell by 38 percent. Bond holders have fared the worst. Today's high interest rates have forced down bond buying and selling prices, which in turn drives the interest rate up since bond prices change in reverse to bond yields.

INFLATION IS HERE TO STAY

Our business community seems to have adopted an inflationary psychology. It expects business recessions (slow-downs), as the one that lasted from 1969 through 1970, to be small and temporary. The slow-downs should then be followed by bigger and better booms. It expects high interest rates and continually rising costs. It believes that higher prices will correct any mistakes caused by overpayment for goods, services, equipment, or capital expansions.

The big worry of government leaders and responsible individuals is that the average consumer is beginning to accept the idea that inflation is a natural part of life. This inflationary psychology is based upon the belief that the smart thing to do is to buy anything that you need now, and to buy it at any cost, because it will never get cheaper. And go into debt to get it, if you must. You will be able to pay off your debts with the higher wages or income you will get later. Today, this inflationary psychology is at work in Brazil, where inflation is considered under control if it does not exceed 35 percent per year! Many people in Brazil get paid daily and spend their evenings hunting for things to buy. In 1924, in the Weimar Republic of Germany, you needed a wheelbarrow full of money to buy one loaf of bread and a billion marks to buy postage for a first class letter. One American dollar would buy 4 trillion marks, and this paper money, with no backing except a defunct government, was used to pay off life insurance policies, savings accounts, mortgages, and other debts. Thus, the lifetime savings of millions of investors were wiped out. Then came a depression; no jobs, no money, only want and hunger. Out of this period came the Nazi dictatorship and finally World War II.

From this example we can see that inflation is one of the biggest dangers now facing Americans and the world. There are ways to stop inflation, or at least to keep it within reasonable bounds. These cures are not popular with politicians because they mean denying voters some of the things they want to own. The main object of a politician is to stay in power, while that of a statesman is to serve. This takes courage, as it is quite often necessary to say, "No, we can't afford this expensive program." If we as a people and a nation can't accept the fact that there has to be a balance between wants and needs and that we must live within our budget, we will be caught in a boom-bust cycle that will end in disaster. All persons, governments, and businesses must live within their means; to do otherwise is financial suicide. The individual also has the opportunity to invest his past labor (in the form of money) as part of a personal system to protect himself against inflation.

You must plan to invest in things that can grow in value along with inflation. These include stocks, raw land, real estate of many different types, businesses, capital goods, equipment, and durable material items such as art, jewelry, books, stamps and coins, and collector items.

We as individuals and as a nation are going to keep on wanting. We will always have dreams and desires. Therefore, one conclusion seems pretty certain: we will continue to have inflation. So you must protect yourself by equity investing.

FORECASTING TOMORROW'S ECONOMY

Foresight is the ability to look into the future and see what lies ahead. The forecasting of business conditions is not a definite science, but it involves an educated guess. Accurate forecasting is one of the major factors necessary for business success. In 1945, the management of Montgomery Ward, the nation's largest retailer, predicted depression after World War II. So they retrenched and saved their cash. Sears, Roebuck & Company, a much smaller company at that time, saw prosperity ahead as consumers had large amounts of money, saved during the war years, and were hungry for all kinds of goods and services. They modernized their management, their stores, and their services.

They expanded and opened many new stores. By 1968 they had a gross volume that was 4 times that of Ward's, who finally merged with another company. This is a graphic example of good economic forecasting. Such forecasting by trained economists is a widely respected management tool used by both government and industry on all levels. These opinions, which are not always right, are used to make hundreds of decisions each day that affect almost everything we do. It is necessary for you to do your own forecasting, and in Chapter 3, you will be given ideas on how to predict your economic future.

SOME CLARIFICATIONS

You have just finished reading the first few pages of this book, and now you are aware that you may need to change your thinking on what an investment is and what it can be. The rest of the book is devoted to giving you some knowledge of what to invest in and how to go about doing it.

This book is not intended as a complete guide on all forms of investing but as a simple, basic introduction to the various fields of investing in which you may hope to make an inflation-proof profit. There is no guarantee that you *will* profit; and in fact, you may sustain a loss. However, I can guarantee that if you keep your money in cashables, you will lose it to inflation.

The word investor in this book refers to both women and men, and can refer to more than one person. Most of the statements describing investments, possibilities for profit or loss, risks involved, and conditions of investing are in general terms. There are many exceptions to any rule, and it is important that you investigate further the field of investing that appeals to you. Only in this manner will you be able to get full information on the investment you are considering and on its possible value for you personally.

2

EVERYONE'S AN INVESTOR

This book is concerned only with investing for monetary gain. As the word "investment" is used in this book, it means an opportunity to increase the capital (money) invested and/or to receive interest (or rent).

There are only four things you can do with your money. You can destroy it, you can spend it, you can invest it, and you can give it away.

THE INVESTOR'S MOTIVES

Consider the ways people can spend their money and call it investing. The kid who spends his dime to buy an ice cream cone is investing in pleasure. The woman who buys a piece of jewelry is investing in vanity. The man who buys a prestige car is investing in pride. The salesman who is selling the car will point to it and say, "That car is a fine investment!" What the salesman is really saying is that the word "investment" means comfort, good looks, pleasure, pride, safety, etc. He does not mean that you can buy the car, go out of the store, and resell it at a profit to increase your capital. You know through experience that the moment you sign the purchase documents, you have lost about $1,000 in depreciation even though you haven't driven the car one foot.

Today there are millions of consumers throughout the world who are investing in material goods because of inflationary psychology (scare buying). Many economists and politicians were surprised by recent powerful economic upsurges caused by heavy consumer buying and its expansive and inflationary effect on the economy. They shouldn't have been surprised; consumers read newspapers and magazines and listen to other communications media. These have been full of stories describing how prices have risen, how they are still rising, and how they will continue to rise in the future. The average consumer, who knows little about investing, has figured out that the only way he can protect himself from inflation is to buy for tomorrow's needs at today's prices. This scare buying has started a consumer spending spree that is helping to drive up prices.

Early in 1969, the federal government took drastic steps to curb inflation by passing laws regulating credit, issuing money restraining orders, and raising taxes. Every investor must be aware that a strong federal government has tremendous economic power and affects every major financial move made in the United States. Yet it took months for government restraints to dampen the economy and to slow the rise in the cost of living as consumers kept on buying to beat higher prices. In the United States, the consumer spending spree has been minor compared to consumer spending in other countries where inflation is 40 percent or more each year.

THE SUCCESSFUL INVESTOR

Now that we have established that everyone is an investor, let's describe what makes a successful, smart, money-oriented investor who will make a profit with his capital.

A successful investor must possess certain personal qualities. There are lucky investors who make spectacular profits once or twice and cannot repeat it, but we are not concerned with luck or with limited successes. We will disregard unusually fortunate outings, as they are duplicated only by chance. We are concerned with rules and aids that can ensure continuous and repeatable successes.

The first personal quality of a successful investor is broad and comprehensive financial knowledge. Since this is something you must have to succeed, the three ways of acquiring it are listed below.

(1) *Serious study.* This requires that you become either a part- or full-time investment professional. You will probably be devoting most of your normal working hours to studying economic reports, investment advisory bulletins, and financial statements and will do your own investment analysis and research. You will probably enroll in a few college courses or take specialized training as offered by brokerage houses, financial institutions, correspondence courses, or lecture series. You may become a licensed real estate broker, registered representative (stock), or management consultant. You may wish to deal with the general public, and thus you will have changed your business or occupation. There are a lot of serious full-time investors, especially in the stock market, who are full-time professionals but have only one client—themselves. Many retired investors are in this category. For these investors any form of investment may be good, as they have the training to evaluate it properly.

(2) *Casual methods.* This involves the use of investment tips and personal friends. Verification of this type of information has to be done by the investor on a spare-time basis. His information comes from generalized popular investment books, magazines, and newspapers. This type of investor has to be very lucky and have extreme patience. His control over his investments generally is quite limited due to his lack of specific knowledge. Most investors fall into this category and should be termed "investment dabblers." If an investor has limited sources of information, he should select reasonably safe investments, such as savings and loan accounts, bank accounts, U.S. Government bonds, certificates of deposit, and life insurance. He should not try to "play" the stock market; many do so to their sorrow.

(3) *Hiring professional advisors.* Those investors who are too limited in time, money, or inclination to increase their financial

knowledge to a professional level can hire the best available investment professional and use his financial ability and knowledge. This is easily accomplished by opening an account with a stock broker or real estate broker, contracting for an investment advisory service, investing in a mutual fund, using the facilities of a full service bank, becoming a partner in a business, buying a franchise operation, etc.

The second personal quality a successful investor must have is good judgment. This is not a trait you can go out and buy like knowledge; it is generally acquired through experience. Judgment can be divided into two main areas. The first is the ability to judge people, and this is by far the hardest. It involves the art of observation: watching, evaluating, and filing away in the mind little pieces of information that, when added together, give a complete picture. You must also weigh the performances of many different people to find the particular person you need for a given action. Capable, efficient, honest personnel is the most important asset of any business or company.

The other area which requires judgment is the evaluation of the general factors influencing a particular investment. Comparisons with other investment possibilities must be fair and not emotionally biased. You must compare such factors as degree of risk, amounts of money and time involved, supervision required, etc. They may turn up investment opportunities in other areas with a greater profit potential. The investor must also judge such aspects of the investment as equipment, buildings, consumer interest, financing, labor, available markets for the product (if any, sales appeal, and sources of supply. This area of facts, figures, and physical property can be judged with close precision. The investor should then be able to make a final judgment of the investment's real potential.

The third personal quality is one that every successful investor needs, and in my opinion it is the most important one. It is also the hardest to acquire. This is the ability to take decisive action at the right moment, including the kind of action involved in turning down an investment under unfavorable conditions. To make a profit by investing, you have to make many important decisions every day. There is constant pressure to act promptly and decisively.

MINIMIZING RISK

There are three time-tested rules for minimizing the investment risk.

The first rule is that every investor should diversify his capital by putting it into several different investments. These may be in the same investment field but should differ in type, value, location, etc. In real estate, you might own several scattered parcels of land; or you might place money in several savings and loan accounts with different companies. Some investors might own life insurance, a bank account, common stock, and perhaps a business. Others may buy a mutual fund for its diversification and then invest in several more funds to get different professional management. If you have all of your investment eggs in one basket, you stand the chance of breaking them all in one accident; so for your financial safety—diversify.

The next rule is to use professional management. This may mean using yourself, your time and ability and education. Or it may mean the use of an attorney, an accountant, a financial advisor, a stock broker, or your banker. It seems a shame that many people ask their barbers for stock market advice or their bankers for legal opinions. You wouldn't ask an auto mechanic to pull an aching tooth, so why not get the financial advice you need from a professional? Paying for such services will turn out to be the best and cheapest action that you, as an investor, can take in the long run.

The third rule is to keep the investment under constant supervision. In my brokerage office we have several clients' mutual fund accounts that are now being held by a custodian bank because neither we nor the mutual fund can locate the client. These clients have moved without leaving forwarding addresses, and they have abandoned thousands of dollars. Fortunately for them, these accounts are not classified as dormant but continue to earn dividends and capital gains and will be fully managed until they are claimed. If an investor abandons a piece of real property, it will sooner or later be seized and sold for taxes. In California, abandoned bank accounts are turned over to the state and, after advertising to find the owners, are finally forfeited to the state if unclaimed. It makes no sense to invest money and then throw it away through lack of interest.

WHAT IS A QUALIFIED INVESTOR?

To sum up, there are nine points that make a qualified investor. He can be defined as a man who:

(1) will spend the necessary time to supervise his investments;

(2) is thoroughly informed about the past performance and future prospects of each investment he owns;

(3) knows enough to read and understand financial statements and to evaluate the progress of the investment;

(4) has a good general knowledge of finance, economics, and business management;

(5) will invest on the basis of sound, objective, unemotional judgment;

(6) keeps up by reading a representative cross section of financial publications, newspapers and magazines, corporation reports, and investment journals;

(7) will give the investment time to develop and not become impatient if it does not follow an ideal schedule;

(8) will respect investing as a full-time business deserving full-time management, not a hobby to be dabbled in or a piece of "action";

(9) will periodically review his investments and compare them objectively with investments in other fields.

If the above qualifications don't fit you, then you must recognize that you are an investment dabbler and not a qualified investor at this point. You have an enjoyable or thrilling hobby, but you are not geared for profit. If you cannot *become* a qualified investor, I suggest you invest in debt equities or a mutual fund, or turn your investments over to an investment manager.

Incidentally, if your spouse is not a qualified investor, I suggest you put your financial house in order so that, in the event of your untimely demise, she (he) will not become a victim of her (his) own financial ignorance. Many spouses have lost estates that would have kept them comfortably for the rest of their lives, by being swindled or following poor advice.

3

INVESTING IN YOUR FUTURE

There are many ways of making money (and I don't mean printing it up in the basement), but the hard part for most of us is to keep it.

Many people want to accumulate a large sum of money in order to pay for a college education for their children. A recent estimate stated that a college education was worth $260,000 in additional income to the college graduate. This extra income generally provides the nicer things in life: bigger cars, world trips, a bigger house, a swimming pool, earlier retirement, more luxurious living. The college graduate moves in higher social circles, his work is more interesting, it can be less physically dangerous. These "fringe" benefits, aside from the income, let one enjoy a better life than when each dollar must be carefully watched. It is estimated that a state college education will cost $14,000 by 1975 and a private college degree about $26,000.

Many people invest in order to buy big-ticket items. These include the luxury automobile, the world cruise, a business, a large home, a boat, or a summer cottage. Such things remain dreams for most people or are achieved only by saving, scrimping, and self-denial or by making a lifetime of payments. With a good financial plan, these dreams can become a reality with relative ease and without hardship.

The U.S. Department of Labor has compiled figures that show the average person owns only his home and some insurance when he reaches age 65—and this is in the richest country in the world! This tragedy could be avoided if people would do some financial planning. Let's look at some statistics on what happens to an average group of 100 men, starting at the age of 25. By age 65, some 36 of them have died; 1 is wealthy, 4 are well-to-do, 5 are self-supporting. The other 54 are dependent on continued work or relatives, friends, and charity. To put it another way, 85 percent of the people who live to 65 have an annual income of less than $2,200.

A retired husband means to most wives twice as much husband on half as much money. Most people, when figuring their retirement needs, plan to cut down on their living costs after retirement by eliminating some items. The problem is which items, and whether they will still be able to afford the necessities after a few years. Most retired people worry that they will outlive their resources and be forced into a home or hospital or reduced to bare subsistence. Out of every 100 persons who live to age 65, 45 will be alive at 80, 24 will make it to 85, and 10 will reach 90 or more. If we assume that you will retire at 65 and live to age 80, then if you spend $400 a month to live, you will spend $72,000 after your income has stopped.

COMPOUNDING RETURNS

If this sounds like an impossible sum to save, let me assure you that every investor has two things going for him automatically. The first is time, and the second is compounding investment returns. These two factors make your task of accumulating wealth much easier than you might think. Any simple plan of investing that includes the reinvestment of profits or income will pleasantly surprise you with its overall results if given enough time.

One illustration of a simple plan that takes almost no effort and yet has shown a superb past performance is the S-4 Keystone Mutual Fund. If you had invested $25 per month ($300 per year) from the beginning of the fund in October 1935, and had reinvested all of the earnings (capital gains) and dividends (interest), your investment would have been worth a total of $128,375 at the end of December, 1970. You would have put in a total of $10,600 to reach this ending value. If you had begun investing in 1950 (putting in a total of $6,000 over the 20-year period and reinvesting all earnings), the ending value would have been $17,756. If you had begun in 1955 (investing $4,500 over 15 years), the ending value would have been $7,528. Beginning in 1958 ($3,000 over 10 years), you would have had an ending value of $3,464. The reason for the tremendous difference in earnings between an investment of $3,000 over 10 years and one of twice that amount over 20 years is that the 20-year investment continues to earn not only on the original capital but on the reinvested returns as well. This is the magic cycle of compounding; you may compound dividends in bank accounts or savings and loans, but in a mutual fund such as the above or in your own business you can also compound earnings (capital gains, which are not a part of simple savings accounts), with a much greater potential return.

In the above illustration of the S-4 mutual fund, no allowance was made for payment of income taxes. Any taxes must be paid out of your income; if you liquidate some of the dividends to pay taxes, the end result will be lowered. The results achieved by the Keystone S-4 Mutual Fund, of course, are a past performance, and there is no assurance that future results will be similar.

Compounding can seem like magic if used right, but it works very simply. If you invest $10, earn 10 percent per year, and add the earnings to the original $10, your investment will grow by $1 the first year to $11; the second year by $1.10 to $12.10; the third year by $1.21 to $13.31; the fourth year by $1.33 to $14.64; and so on. The amount accelerates faster each year as the investment capital is increased by the reinvestment of the earnings.

ESTIMATION OF YOUR MONEY NEEDS

Let's use the problem of retirement and estimate that you are planning to retire in 15 years. First, list the fixed costs you will be paying at retirement time. These would include mortgage payments, insurance, etc., and these costs would remain constant. Then there are the items for which costs will rise slightly over the years, such as telephone, health insurance, gas, lights, and water. Last come the necessities, such as food, drugs, clothing, and transportation. These items will vary in monthly dollar amounts and will also show a rising cost pattern over the years. Next come the luxuries, such as entertainment, dining out, travel, gifts for the children or grandchildren, an occasional beer or ball game, and the like. These luxuries may have to be eliminated if there isn't enough money, and they are the difference between living and just existing.

One way to estimate your retirement money needs is to calculate your present living costs and then adapt them to your anticipated needs at age 65 by cutting out whatever will be unnecessary at that time. Compute these costs at today's prices to get today's retirement cost. Multiply that figure by 1.7 to compensate for 3.5 percent inflation over the 15-year period. If today's retirement figure is $300 per month, then $300 multiplied by 1.7 is $510—the amount you will need 15 years from now.

If you are eligible for Social Security, you can estimate that the retirement benefits will be raised about 3.5 percent per year also. In the previous edition we used the maximum rate of benefits based on $500 in earnings which would have paid $162 for a single person or $252 for a couple. Congress seems to raise the benefits and taxes every few years, so in 1970, on a $650 base earnings, the benefit would be $230 for a single person or $345 for a couple. The difference between what you can expect from Social Security and your estimated needs must come from retirement benefits from your company, your investments, or from cutting your budget and doing without.

To compute the amount of invested capital you will need, you may use the following formula: divide the annual income you will need from investments by an assumed rate of return (interest?). The higher the estimated rate of return, the smaller the amount of invested capital required. For example, if you need an extra $3,000 from investments and you figure you can get 6 percent on your money, then $3,000 divided by 0.06 is $50,000, the required capital.

To sum it up, if your budget calls for $600 per month or $7,000 per year, and Social Security is $400 per month or $4,800 per year, the difference is $7,200 minus $4,800, or $2,400 needed. $2,400 divided by 0.06 is $40,000; this is the required capital to generate the needed $2,400 at 6 percent interest.

To have $40,000 in capital in 15 years, you would have to invest $147 a month at a 5 percent compound interest rate. If you could raise the rate of return from a savings and loan rate of 5 percent to, say, 9 percent (which some mutual funds can show), then you would have to invest only $125 per month.

Now comes the big decision. Where should I put my present investment dollars to earn as much as possible with the least amount of risk?

It is my belief that the age of the investor is a very important factor. A young man who has sufficient income to pay his living costs should invest in speculative situations without considering any current return on his money. He should be able to live and invest part of his wages.

As the investor grows older and has family responsibilities, he is justified in putting part of his money into less speculative investments and/or balancing them out with solid growth investments. This switching is done as a hedge against losing part of what he has accumulated and for peace of mind. The older person, who is close to or already in retirement should have all of his capital invested in good quality income-producing investments that will provide both income and protection against inflation.

It can be safely stated that in the future you will walk through the door of the place where you make a living for the last time. Death, sickness, accident, retirement, company bankruptcy, job loss—all of these mean you will have to have a second income to replace today's income, which will be gone.

TYPES OF RISKS TO BE CONSIDERED IN INVESTMENT PLANNING

In my opinion, every investment has some element of risk. It makes no difference whether the investment is in U.S. Government bonds or in oil well wildcatting. You, as an intelligent investor, must weigh the amount of risk against the possible profit. You can have a good investment only when the possibilities of profit exceed the possibilities of loss. For example, if a $25 share of stock has a potential loss of $5 and a potential profit of $15, the profit ratio is 3 to 1. If other things are equal, then in my judgment it would be a good investment. This is the risk of capital gain or capital loss. This type of risk (numbers) is present in any investment where there is no guarantee that the invested dollars will be returned.

If you bought some stock for $1,000 and sold it for $500, you had a capital loss. If you sold it for $1,500, there was a capital gain.

The second form of risk is the loss of purchasing power or inflation. Over long spans of time this risk of loss becomes a certainty, as prices are and have been on a long-term upward trend. For example, if you had invested $1,000 in a savings and loan account in January, 1958, and had taken it out in December, 1973, your original capital of $1,000 would buy only $400 worth of goods, and this is a loss due to inflation.

TYPES OF INVESTMENT

There are actually only two types of investment: debt and equity.

In debt investment, the investor loans his capital to others and charges them interest (rent). As the investor loans the money, he will generally loan it at a rate that varies with the safety of his invested capital. Government bonds are backed by the general credit of the government. Corporate bonds can be backed by the corporation's general credit or by pledging some of the corporation's material assets or income as collateral. If you purchase bonds, debentures, or mortgages, deposit (loan) your money in a bank account or a savings and loan account, or make a personal loan, then you have made a debt investment.

If you invest in shares of stock, land, buildings, property, stamps, coins, or a business, you have become the owner of an equity investment. After any expenses such as loans made, insurance, fees, licenses, overhead, and labor have been paid, the income remaining is the owner's profit (if any). If the equity is too large for one investor, as in a corporation like General Motors, there may be many owners, perhaps even hundreds of thousands, who will share in the profit or loss of the corporation according to the number of shares they own.

CALCULATION OF INVESTMENT RETURN

Many investors do not know how to figure the rate of return on an investment. If 10 years ago you bought 100 shares of stock for $1,000 and received a dividend of $50, the yield was 5 percent. This is the rate of return on the original investment at the then current market value. If the dividend has been raised so that it currently pays $400, many investors would feel that they are currently receiving a 40 percent return on their investment. If the price of the shares is still $1,000, this is true; but if the shares are valued at any other price, the current rate of return will be different.

For example, if the shares have risen to a current value of $10,000 and pay a $400 dividend, the current yield (return) would be only 4 percent. You must use today's market value (the price for which you could sell the shares) as the actual amount you have invested. The original price has nothing to do with computing what you are actually receiving from your current investment; it would be like comparing eggs and oranges. Today's selling value is $10,000; you could sell your stock, reinvest that amount in something like a bank savings account, and receive $500 per year if the bank pays 5 percent.

PERSONAL PROBLEMS IN INVESTING

The most important problem to solve is the emotional problem of risk. I suggest that you ask yourself, "Will it bother me if I lose all or even part of what I have in this investment?" If the loss would cause you great regret, sleeplessness, or undue worry, you should not make the investment. The more a loss would damage your peace of mind, the more conservative your investments should be. If the thought of loss really bothers you then you should stick to U.S. Government bonds, insured savings and loan accounts, certificates of deposit, bank accounts, and life insurance. These debt investments offer safety of capital, and in most cases they are either guaranteed or insured against loss.

We discussed earlier the relationship of investing to age, but peace of mind is important at any age. Another problem is patience. Many investors have taken a "bath" because they invested and then sold out before the investment had a chance to mature. How many times have you heard someone say "Gee, I owned that but I sold out long before it went up in value"? Generally, when we make an investment we expect a certain result and set up a mental time schedule. If the result takes longer than we anticipate or does not follow our schedule, we become unhappy and look for an excuse to sell out. Selling on this basis is emotional and doesn't show knowledge or good judgment.

Many other investors who cannot stand the thought of loss will stick with an investment when it is falling in value, waiting for it to go back up so they can break even. This attitude in the stock market explains why so many investors suffer heavy losses; they refuse to take their licking, get out, and reinvest in something that has a better possibility for profit. Others will ride an investment up and won't sell because they expect it to go still higher and they want to wring the last dollar of profit by selling out at the top. Both of these investors are controlled by greed, and unless they are willing to subordinate greed to judgment based on knowledge, they will always lose.

Retirement preparation means planning the use of your leisure time, the place for retirement, and the amount of money you will need to pay the bills. I have tried to point out that you and I like the finer things in life. We are looking forward to enjoying the marvelous new things that we know are coming. We know that we will need more dollars in the future for our living costs. If you cannot invest in a field where you are an expert, you must trust your capital to someone who *is* an expert in whom you can place your trust.

This book is basically oriented to people 30 to 60, and you are urged to devote your energies to building up your capital in the 5 to 35 income-producing years you have left. There are dozens of ways to invest your money. All of these investment paths have lead some investors to greater wealth. One of them can do the same for you.

In the following chapters, you will find a plan that you can use. It will help you select the right investment for your particular financial needs.

Don't you think that now is the time for you to get your share of the wealth that is on this earth? Your fair and just share?

Read on, for the time has come to stop wishing and day-dreaming. You can start making money the easy way, by investing and letting others work for you.

4

DEBT INVESTING

Probably the most common kind of investment, the one used by most people, is debt investing; this includes the purchase of bonds, bank or savings and loan accounts, credit union membership, and the like.

BONDS

A bond is an evidence of a loan made to the issuer of the bond. Basically it is an I.O.U. or a promissory note with a face value of $1,000. Bonds are also issued in amounts of $100 and $500. Bonds promise to pay a specified interest rate for a specified time period, plus the face value at maturity.

Bonds are issued by corporations, foundations, national governments, and smaller political subdivisions such as states, counties, cities, special districts, etc. A secured bond or a mortgage bond is backed by a lien on real property owned by the issuer which can be seized by the bondholder if the issuer fails to meet the terms of the bond. An income bond's interest is paid out of available income, while a revenue bond pays its interest from general revenue. If money is set aside to redeem bonds before the maturity date, they are called sinking fund bonds.

Coupon bonds have coupons attached which are clipped off

and presented to the issuer's paying office for the interest earned on the due date. This is where the expression "sit on your backside and do nothing but clip coupons" came from. Coupon bonds are bearer bonds which are freely tradeable, since they are not registered but are payable to the bearer (whoever has them in his possession). When the owner is named on the bond, it is called a registered bond, and ownership must be changed when the bond is sold or traded.

A debenture is a bond that is backed only by the general credit of the issuer. Many debentures are subordinated to other obligations owed by the bond's issuer, and the bondholder in buying has agreed to waive his claim to interest or principal until any such obligations are paid. Bond investors must watch very closely for any subordinating clauses.

Rising interest rates and inflation have created a popular demand for the convertible bond. These bonds can be exchanged under specified conditions for a specified number of either preferred or common shares in the issuing company. This is advantageous for the bondholder, as he can earn interest even though the stock of the issuer pays no dividends. In inflation, or if the price of the common stock rises, the bond holder can share, through the convertible feature, in any rise in the market price of the issuer's stock.

Many bonds are now being traded at a discount (below face value) because the specified interest rate is too low. Bond yields vary with the market price. A $1,000 bond that has a 4 percent interest rate pays $40 per year. If the bond is now selling for $800, the current yield is $40 divided by $800, or 5 percent. If the bond is now selling for $1,200, then the current yield is $40 divided by $1,200, or 3.33 percent. Bonds are also described as having a "yield to maturity." If the 4 percent bond were bought for $1,000 and held 10 years to maturity, it would yield 4 percent to maturity. If the bondholder paid $800 for it, he would have a $200 capital gain in 10 years. $200 divided by 10 years is 2 percent, plus the 5 percent current yield would give a yield to maturity of 7 percent. If the same bond were purchased for $1,200, the yield to maturity would be a $200 loss in 10 years, or minus 2 percent, plus 3.33 percent current interest—a total of 1.33 percent.

Bond yields go up when the bond falls in price, and the yields go down when the price goes up. You can find bond prices quoted in the larger daily papers or *The Wall Street Journal.* The calculation of bond prices and yields is fairly complicated, so it is best to check with a stock broker or a bank and let them show you how bond pricing works.

Corporate bonds are generally offered on a dollar basis, and government bonds are offered on a yield basis. Bonds are generally sold by the issuer to an underwriting group of stock brokers or banks on a bid basis. Bond bidding may call for the buying of $150 million in bonds at one time, so it is big business that needs expert financial knowledge. Most bond offerings have a small percentage profit in them for the underwriters. If the underwriters are not able to move the bonds "off the shelf" they may have to cut the reoffering price and take a loss. Most bonds are traded in specialty brokerage houses called "bond houses."

KINDS OF BONDS

Corporations issue bonds to gain working capital or funds for investing, capital expenditures, equipment, etc. Bonds are favored by banks, railroads, and finance companies. They enable the issuer to raise money without diluting the shareholder's ownership.

Government bonds are actually debentures, as they are backed by the full authority of the government and its right to impose taxes. They are secured only by the general credit of the government. They are usually issued to finance capital expenditures, and sometimes to pay operating expenses.

U.S. Government bonds are issued in many different series; Treasury bonds are issued with a face value of $1,000 and are freely tradeable. They are issued for periods of more than 5 years. They may be used for collateral and their interest is fully taxed. The price at which they trade varies from day to day according to current interest rates. Many government bonds issued years ago with interest rates as low as 2 or 3 percent can now be purchased at a discount as high as 40 percent ($600 for a $1,000 bond!).

U.S. Treasury bills are issued for periods up to 90 days. U.S. Treasury notes are issued for periods of 1 to 6 years. Both of these issues may be purchased at government auctions, or a service bank will buy them for you for a flat fee of $25 for $100,000 or less. Treasury bonds are traded by stock brokers, banks, and bond houses.

The safety of capital (numbers) is highest if held until maturity, while the safety from inflation is low. The investor faces the probability of loss of capital if interest rates rise.

Treasury issues are recommended for corporations who wish to keep their money working and earning but in a liquid investment for easy convertibility into cash. They are excellent for their high collateral value and for capital safety. Individuals will find them a good long-term holding when safety of capital is desired more than protection against inflation.

Municipal bonds or debentures are issued by counties, cities, and states. The market value varies daily according to interest rates, grade of the bond, and investor demand. The grade or rating of the bond depends upon the financial industry's evaluation and its confidence in the ability of the issuing government to pay the specified interest and the principal amount when due. Municipal bonds have been issued by very small governmental units far in excess of their ability to pay. Many times these bonds are issued to raise revenues to buy land, put in roads, sewers, and pipelines, erect industrial plants, etc. The industrial plants are offered to corporations on a lease, or even rent-free, in order to bring new industry to the community and create wealth, jobs, and prosperity.

If the company occupying the industrial plant moves, quits, or goes broke, the bond may default, and the bondholder will probably suffer a large if not total loss. Municipal bonds are presently exempt from federal income taxes, so they are an excellent source of tax-free income for people who pay 35 percent or more income tax. If a municipal bond pays 5 percent interest, a taxpayer in the 50 percent income tax bracket would have to have a taxable investment return of 10 percent to equal it. As municipal bonds depend upon federal tax laws and there is considerable agitation to tax municipal bond interest, it is possible that such interest will be taxed in the future. If this happens, the face value of municipal bonds will fall as wealthy people turn to other investments with a higher rate of return even if fully taxable.

U.S. SAVINGS BONDS

Investors hold $62.5 billion of E & H savings bonds as of June, 1974. They are issued by the U. S. Treasury Department. Freedom Shares, a short-term variety of these bonds, were discontinued June, 1970 but they continue to draw interest at 6 percent.

The interest rate on these bonds is set by the U. S. Congress, and they have raised the rate of interest several times. The last rate increase was made effective Dec., 1973 and went to 6 percent on all bonds including older ones already outstanding. This means you get 6 percent even if the bond has a different rate on it or the maturity date is long past due. Remember, old bonds are valuable, so don't throw them away! The first bonds were issued in May, 1941 at 2.9 percent and were called Defense Bonds. It was stated that the rate would be raised and it was from 4¼ to 6 percent. They are now comparable to bank savings accounts and savings and loan shares.

These debt securities cannot be sold, transferred, or used for collateral. They may be redeemed after being held for an initial 2-month period.

While the interest limitation keeps the yield lower than that of other investments, there are many advantages in owning savings bonds. They are registered in the name of the buyer, so they are easily replaced if lost, stolen, or damaged. E Bond interest may be reported for federal income tax purposes either as it is earned or when the bond is redeemed, at the investor's option. The interest received is free from any state or local income taxes.

They are easy to purchase, as they are available at banks, savings and loans, and post offices. Many companies have a payroll deduction plan. This is a convenient way for the investor to save money, since it is deducted before he receives his paycheck and therefore is generally not missed. E bonds are issued at cost, and the interest is added on at the end of each 6-month period after the bond's initial purchase date. They range in cost from $18.75 for a $25 face value bond to $7,500 for a $10,000 bond.

In 1973 inflation was 10.8 percent, while the interest paid was only 6 percent. So the investor who had savings bonds lost 4.8 percent of his capital to inflation. If he paid any income tax on the interest earned, the amount paid in taxes was an additional loss.

These bonds are backed by the full taxing power of the United States Government. Therefore they are one way to preserve the investor's capital against loss of numbers. Savings Bonds and Freedom Shares are recommended for those investors who need a systematic and painless plan for accumulating wealth, such as a bank or payroll deduction plan. It is a preferred investment for any investor who would worry about losing a portion of his capital.

COMMERCIAL PAPER

Commercial paper is the name for short-term notes that mature in 5 to 180 days, although they are sometimes available up to 360 days. They are issued by corporations such as General Finance, Budget Finance, General Motors Acceptance Corporation, Penney Stores; etc. They are backed by the general credit of the company and therefore do not have any specific collateral. At the end of June, 1974, there was over $41 billion worth of commercial paper issued to investors.

It is a popular method of financing for corporations, who may thus acquire money for short-term needs without being involved in any expensive or involved financing procedures such as issuing stock or debentures, trying to find a secured loan, or mortgaging some specific piece of real estate. Commercial paper is very easily

Commercial papers of Corp's.
@ 25,000

issued. The money is available to the issuing corporation the same day or at most within two days. The issuance of commercial paper has added advantages, in that it does not change or disturb the overlap corporate financial structure, nor does it need the approval of the corporation's shareholders.

It is beneficial to investors to buy commercial paper; they may earn interest on money that ordinarily would be idle for a period of a few days or even months.

These short-term notes are generally sold in amounts of $25,000 or more. Interest-bearing notes are sold at face value, and interest is paid at the maturity date. Discounted notes are also sold, and when the interest is added at maturity the note is redeemed at face value. Both types of notes are calculated to pay the same interest rate. The risk element is small if the investor buys commercial paper that is issued by large "blue chip" corporations.

Investors who go to the trouble of making inquiries about the availability of these notes, buying them, picking up and delivering checks and notes, will find it worth the effort. Generally speaking, but especially in a "tight" money market, commercial paper pays a higher interest rate than is paid on a bank savings account or a savings and loan account. Currently the maximum bank rate is 5 percent on bank certificates of deposit, and California savings and loan accounts pay 5.25 percent. At the same time the interest rate paid on commercial paper is 5.5 percent. You can see that the interest paid on commercial paper is considerably more than you can realize from a savings and loan account.

Investing in these short-term notes is especially profitable for small corporations who would like to employ their money for short periods and not leave it idle in a checking account. Separate reserve accounts, such as those set up for depreciation, inventory, tax reserves, etc., can be used to earn interest and still be readily available when needed.

To find out what commercial paper is available in your area, you may inquire at a stock broker or full service bank, or check the larger corporations and finance companies directly.

SAVINGS AND LOAN ACCOUNTS

Savings and Loan (S & L) accounts are a debt equity; the

depositor (investor) is loaning his money to the S & L for interest only. Even though many S & L accounts have provisions for bonus interest rates if funds are left undisturbed for three or more years, it should be clearly understood by the depositor that his money on deposit does not put him in line for any other "profits." Dividends may be paid out to shareholders of record, but being a depositor does not make one a shareholder, only owning S & L stock can accomplish that.

The S & L institutions relend the depositor's money to borrowers who wish to purchase real estate. The S & L's hold first mortgages as a lien on any real estate for their loan. As an S & L account is a debt investment, the investor has a guarantee that he will be able to get the same numbers of dollars out as he put in when the account is liquidated. Most S & L associations belong to the Federal Home Loan Bank System, and these accounts are insured up to $20,000 each against capital loss by the Federal Savings & Loan Insurance Corporation, a government agency.

For personal safety, many investors who have more than $20,000 open several accounts in different S & L's under different names, such as their wives' names, children's names, joint accounts, etc. This enables them to have the full $20,000 insurance on each account. In 1970 there were over 45 million persons who had S & L accounts, and over 10 million people had borrowed from them.

While S & L accounts have excellent capital safety, they have not fared too well in recent years when compared to other types of investment, because of inflation. If you had opened both an S & L account and an ICA Mutual Fund account on January 1, 1956 for $10,000 each, you would have received $6,130 in S & L dividends and $7,004 in ICA Mutual Fund dividends. On December 31, 1970, 15 years after opening the accounts, the S & L account would have a dollar value of $10,000 and the ICA Mutual Fund of $28,535 (which includes the reinvestment of declared capital gains). The S & L account's purchasing power would be $7,593, a loss of 24 percent, or 2.4 percent per year, of invested capital. The ICA Mutual Fund would have a purchasing power of $46,366, or a gain of 46 percent per year. In 1970, the California S & L's paid 5¼ percent interest and the U.S.

Bureau of Labor Statistics Consumer Price Index showed inflation was 5.3 percent. Therefore, the net investment loss was 0.05 percent. Since the average depositor pays income taxes, and S & L interest is taxable, the S & L depositor in 1970 actually lost purchasing power on his invested capital in what is really a very conservative investment. This points out the fact that all investments involve risk when purchasing power is considered.

The money borrowed from the depositor by the S & L's is generally invested in mortgages on single-family dwellings. Additional income is generated by the S & L's from escrow loan and appraisal fees, drawing document charges, etc. When the S & L's are able to loan money on mortgages at a rate that is 1.75 percent higher than the interest paid, they should be able to operate profitably.

The "dividends" (actually interest) paid are usually higher in the Western part of the U.S. as there is more competition for the S & L dollar and less money available than in other parts of the country. This is why you will see advertisements in national magazines telling of the higher rates which attract mortgage money to the West. S & L accounts are very easy to open and many are opened by mail. Many S & L's have a bonus of ¾ of 1 percent for accounts that are held 3 years or more. Interest rates are set by the Federal Home Loan Bank.

Savings and loans are either stock or mutual companies. Mutual S & L's are chartered by the Federal Government. In theory, they are owned by the depositors and the borrowers. However, most mutual S & L's have proxies printed on the signature cards or buried in one of the loan documents. This enables the present management to run the S & L as their private domain. There is seldom any publicity regarding the annual meeting, so management decisions are not debated and the management is able to perpetuate itself without challenge.

Stock company S & L's are owned by the shareholders or are subsidiaries of a holding company. The shareholders are notified of the annual meeting and generally have a semi-annual report furnished them. Management can be questioned and can be voted out of office by a majority of the shareholders. Stock S & L's are generally held by a holding company which may also own an escrow company, bank, insurance agency, construction company, etc. Some holding companies should be termed "integrated financial empires." Lincoln Financial Corporation is an example, and its stock is traded in over-the-counter markets. Both types offer the same safety features and have the same degree of safety.

S & L popularity as a place to save has enabled many persons to buy homes who would not have been able to borrow from banks with their strict loan policies. While there has been loud protest from borrowers and politicians about high mortgage rates, these high rates have enabled S & L's to pay higher interest and encourage prudent people to save.

I would recommend S & L accounts as a convenient place to invest some funds for emergency use. However, the yield is not high enough for the average investor to make his capital grow in purchasing power. S & L accounts are convenient, safe, and easy to open, and funds are generally available on short notice.

BANK ACCOUNTS

Bank savings accounts are also a debt equity. They are very easy to open and the depositor's money is available for withdrawal without notice. Interest rates range from 0.5 to 1.5 percent less than that paid by S & L's. Most banks are members of the Federal Depositors Insurance Corporation, so savings accounts are insured up to $20,000 each.

One of the popular features offered by most banks is an automatic transfer of money from non-interest-paying checking accounts into savings accounts. This investor convenience enables depositors to save money on a "painless" plan.

Most banks offer "Christmas savings plans" so depositors may save a few dollars each week to have money to spend for Christmas. Surveys have found that less than half of the depositors complete the plan. Most people transfer these savings to their regular savings accounts. Most of these plans pay little or no interest and in my opinion are one of the poorest excuses for an investment existing today. For your own sake, use a regular savings account if you save at a bank. Don't give the bank the use of your money without charging them for it.

CREDIT UNIONS

A credit union is a cooperative association of persons with a common bond of occupation or association; or it can be a group of people who live in a well-defined area such as a rural community. Federal credit unions are charted and supervised by the Bureau of Federal Credit Unions, a part of the U.S. Department of Health, Education, and Welfare. Other credit unions are chartered by the appropriate state government. Massachusetts passed the first credit union law in 1909, and the Federal Credit Union Act was passed in 1934. Today, some 18 million people have over $11 billion in more than 22,300 credit unions.

Since half of all credit unions are federally chartered, and most state chartered ones are quite similar, the following statistics and facts apply to both types.

Besides meeting the common bond or residence membership requirements, members have to pay a membership fee of 25¢. This can be a big bargain if you are eligible for a well-run credit union. Since credit unions were designed to encourage thrift, most will take a deposit of 25¢ or more. Deposits by investors are described in shares, and each share represents $5 in the account. The Board of Directors may require a 2-month notice for withdrawal of funds. Starting January 1, 1970 up to $20,000 per account is insured. Actual statistics for the past 30 years have shown that uncollectible loan losses have been consistently about 2/10ths of 1 percent (20¢ per $100 of loans), which is a remarkable safety record.

Credit unions are managed by a Board of Directors and a credit committee whose members serve on an annual basis, without pay, and are elected each year by the credit union's membership. The Board of Directors elects the officers. Only the treasurer is authorized to be paid if the membership so votes. Officers and directors serve in these time-consuming jobs as an unselfish service for their friends and neighbors.

Loans can be made only to the members of the credit union, regardless of the number of shares they have. Loan applications must be approved by the credit committee. Loans can be made for a maximum of 10 years. Unsecured salary loans are limited to $2,500. Interest charges have a maximum limit of 1 percent per month, which includes any fees. Secured loans or larger loans generally have an interest charge of 8/10ths of 1 percent per month (9.6 percent per year).

Credit unions' earnings come from interest collected on member's loans, fees, and interest from surplus funds. The surplus funds must be invested in insured Savings & Loans, in U.S. Treasury Bonds and bills or securities of U.S. Agencies, such as Fanny Maes.

At the end of each 6-month period the Board of Directors declares the amount of the interest rate to be paid on the credit union shares held for the past 6 months. By law, credit unions cannot pay more than 6 percent interest. Many paid 5 or 5.5 percent in 1970. 20 percent of the credit union's net earnings and any surplus undistributed profit are set aside in a reserve fund to cover uncollectible loan losses. Many credit unions furnish group credit insurance that pays any loan balance if the borrower dies or becomes totally and permanently disabled.

For further information on investing in or starting a credit union, you may write the National Credit Union Administration, Washington, D.C. 20456.

We recommend that limited amounts be placed in credit unions as emergency funds. It establishes your credit for low-cost loans and it enables the beginning investor to save a regular amount out of each paycheck, even if the amount is very small. It is a very sensible place to save.

5

LIFE INSURANCE

A life insurance policy is a contract that will pay to the policyholder specified benefits at the end of a specified period of time. It is a system for protecting yourself from financial disaster in case of death by making a small payment based not on "individual risk," but on the statistical "group certainty" of a calculated average number of deaths.

By signing the insurance form, you can create an instant estate or supply of money for your beneficiaries. There is no other method of creating an estate with the stroke of a pen. In 1969, the Institute of Life Insurance estimated that the average American family had $19,500 in life insurance protection, which was an increase from $17,200 in 1967. This amount of protection is equivalent to three years of after-tax income.

Through common usage the term "life insurance" has come to include group insurance, income, accident, travel, and health coverage, annuities, etc. But the strict meaning should be limited to insurance that pays a benefit on the death of the policyholder, and the term will be so used in this chapter. Life insurance can be divided into two categories: protection and investment. However, there is no single investment that can guarantee both wealth and security. Every person who has a financial plan should include enough insurance to provide for the unexpected. I believe that everyone needs an accident and health policy to provide income when disabled. A medical policy should be owned to pay for the constantly rising costs of hospitals and doctors.

WHAT INSURANCE DO YOU NEED?

The need for life insurance protection depends upon the individual's family responsibilities. Persons without dependents have little need for life insurance unless they wish to be sure they will be insurable in the future. The family man with small children, especially when the wife is not trained to work, needs the maximum amount of insurance he can afford. When the head of the family dies there is a triple loss: of the wage-earner, of the husband, and of the father. It is the loss of the wage-earner that can cause financial disaster. To prevent this disaster, I believe that all, or almost all, of the life insurance carried by each family should be on the wage-earner. Insurance on dependents should be limited to small amounts intended to pay the final expenses of death.

Many times I have heard of men dying who have let their own life insurance policies lapse, but have kept a college plan for the kids. These policies on the children's lives will not get them through college; the policies' values are usually too small to cover college costs. Probably they will lapse, since the mother has the problem of trying to feed and clothe the children until they are college age or can start earning for themselves. With the advent of modern financial planning and a widespread knowledge of insurance and investments by the public, many enlightened life insurance companies are going back to the basic principle of life insurance and the job that they can do better than anyone else—providing protection.

Today, almost all wage-earners can afford to carry a term life insurance policy of $100,000 or more. This is a small enough estate to leave dependents in today's economy, where prices are rising so fast, to provide them with a reasonable standard of living until the children are grown or the beneficiary is ready for retirement. As the children grow up and go off into the world on their own, the need for insurance protection lessens, and the emphasis turns to acquiring wealth for later use with some protection. To solve this problem the life insurance industry has developed combination protection and investment policies such as the endowment plan, which pays the policy's face value at age 65 in cash.

Life insurance is an economic and social necessity. A life insurance policy, however, is a social device that is often badly used, unfairly sold, and only slightly understood by most policyholders in the United States. We have developed the most efficient and determined sales force known to man to sell life insurance. These salespeople are taught to sell their product aggressively on the basis of emotional appeal and social conscience. In one common approach, a prospect is shown a graduation-day picture with a boy and a girl in cap and gown. They are telling their friends that their Dad had the foresight to provide a college education for them. The prospect is a blanked-out figure in the picture.

These effective salesmen created a need by painting a word picture, then sell you their services to fill the need. They work on a commission basis; most of them prefer to sell high-premium policies that pay higher commissions to them and earn more for the company. Through comprehensive training, life insurance companies have instilled a high degree of loyalty and the acceptance of company methods.

TYPES OF LIFE INSURANCE COMPANIES

One major type of life insurance company is the mutual company, owned (in theory) by the policyholders. They have the right to elect officers and directors and to establish company procedures. But since proxies are built into the policy, about the only thing the mutual policyholder really gets is the annual report telling of the company's progress or giving excuses for the lack of it!

The other major type of company is the old line legal reserve company. These are owned by shareholders, who need not be policyholders. They have the same rights as stockholders in any other corporation, but generally the public has only a small part of the issued stock. I feel that the ownership of stock in a life insurance company is one of the most profitable long-term investments you can buy.

Much has been said about the safety of life insurance companies. Let's go back to the big depression of 1929 and see how they actually fared. At the time of the banking moratorium in March, 1933, the banks were closed for one week for inspection of their books. If the banks had more assets than liabilities and could pay off their depositors, they were allowed to reopen, resume normal business, and accept additional deposits. At the same time as the bank moratorium, a 6-month moratorium on life insurance companies was declared which lasted to September, 1933, and later in some states.

This moratorium was declared only on banking obligations and the payment of cash and loan values of existing policies. The life insurance companies were allowed to go right on selling new policies, paying agent's commissions, and accepting premiums as usual. At the same time, the companies were denying their policyholders the right to be paid for just and fairly contracted obligations. Hundreds of millions of dollars worth of life insurance policies were cancelled because policyholders could not pay their premiums.

The Best Life Insurance Report of 1940 states that more than $200 million in cash values were lost by policyholders. This is the actual record, despite statements you may have heard or read that say something like, "No one has ever lost one penny of his savings in a life insurance company."

You will find that mutual companies generally charge slightly higher premiums than legal reserve companies for the same policies. Policies are sold on either a dividend-paying basis or a non-participating (no dividend) basis. Since dividends are nothing more than the refund of an overcharge, it is more sensible to buy a non-participating policy.

If a mutual life insurance company becomes insolvent it may be sold, or the insurance in force may be sold to another company, or the company may assess each policyholder his proportionate share of the deficit. If a legal reserve company becomes insolvent it may produce additional financial reserves (generally by selling additional stock) or by making a long-term loan. It may sell its insurance in force to another company, or it may merge with another, stronger life insurance company. If the policies are sold or the company is merged, there is no change in premiums or policy benefits. Leroy A. Lincoln, President of Metropolitan Life, the world's largest life insurance company, said in 1949 (and the statement is just as valid today): "You're as safe, as well protected, and the cost is just as cheap if you buy from a small insurance company as from the largest."

A HARD LOOK AT INSURANCE

Now let us look at life insurance in an objective manner and not the way it would be described by a selling agent.

(1) "Cash values in policies belong to you, the policyholder." This is sheer bunk; you can only get the cash value by surrendering the policy and giving up your insurance to get "your money." Or you can borrow "your cash value" and pay interest on it! Can you imagine going down to your bank, asking for your savings, and having the banker say, "Sure we'll give you your money, but we will charge you interest; and of course we'll deduct the interest first!" You would think this was robbery and call for the police! Yet we have let the life insurance industry get away with this lie for years.

(2) Life insurance policies cannot insure the policyholder and provide a competitive savings program. It can do only one job, and that is to pay, when the policyholder dies, a sum of money to his beneficiaries. Since life insurance proceeds are guaranteed, the insurance companies must use policy benefits which have been calculated on very low rates of interest on the cash reserves that back up the policies. Most life insurance companies compute policy reserve estimates at 2.5 or 3 percent, which does not even keep up with the way inflation devalues money. This is why life insurance cannot be considered a good investment—unless you expect to die during the first few years and consider the amount

by which the death benefits exceed the premium as a profit. This is the hard way to profit, and I would not recommend it.

(3) All life insurance is term insurance. Level premium policies that have a cash value are actually decreasing term policies. As the cash value of a policy increases every year, the actual amount of insurance at risk declines. This means that the life insurance company's insurance liability decreases each year until the cash value equals the face value of the policy. For example, if a $5,000 face value policy has in the 5th year a cash value of $200, the company is risking $4,800 in insurance. If the cash value rises in 10 years to $2,000, the company is furnishing $3,000 in insurance. If in the 19th year the cash value is $4,500, the company has a $500 insurance liability. So in the end, the policyholder will buy his own life insurance with his cash values and the life insurance company will finally be relieved of all insurance liability.

(4) In all level premium policies with cash values, the cost per $1,000 of life insurance will go up as the cash values increase. If you paid a $100 premium for the $5,000 policy in the first year, you would have paid $20 per thousand. In the 5th year you are paying the same $100 for $4,800 in insurance, which is $20.81 per thousand. In the 10th year, you are paying a $100 premium for $3,000 in insurance, or $33.34 per thousand; and in the 19th year, you are paying $100 for $500 in insurance, or $200 per thousand! Therefore, no one can say that a $5,000 life insurance policy, has a permanent of $5,000 nor can any other cash value policy be considered as permanent insurance, not when the value decreases.

(5) The only actual benefit an insurance policy can provide is a death benefit. Any return of premiums is a fictitious savings. Many policies are gimmicked up with a mixture of insurances or additional riders to hide this fact. For example, you can buy a policy that will be paid up at age 65 with a rider that will provide additional insurance to cover all of the premiums paid. This is a combination policy that has great sales appeal, in that it offers you "free" insurance or promises that you'll recover all monies paid at death. It is actually a sales gimmick to sell an additional amount of insurance. Combinations such as these are put together

by the life insurance companies as sales tools to overcome objections, whether obvious or not, by prospective policy holders.

(6) Premiums paid in advance, which include the higher premiums collected in the early days of the policy, are not savings even though referred to as such by the companies.

(7) There is no such thing as an insurance dividend. The Bureau of Internal Revenue treats it as a return of capital (an overcharge) and therefore it is not taxable. Buying a policy for its dividends is buying back your own money with quite a lot of it deducted to pay the company's expenses.

To sum it all up, insurance policies are written for the policyholder's protection, but so that the company can profit as much as possible. There is nothing wrong with a profit, but why not keep it for yourself?

PREMIUMS

How is an insurance premium determined? The first cost item is the net basic premium. This is found by the use of a life expectancy (mortality) table. If the insurance company covers enough people, it does not matter to them who dies, just how many. It is an inescapable fact that as each year passes we all get a little closer to our ultimate end, death. The number of people who are expected to die, divided by the number of those who are living at the beginning of the year, gives a death rate figure that becomes the net basis premium after the expected interest earned by the paid premium is subtracted. To this figure is added business overhead, expenses, salesmen's commissions, taxes, and reserves. Policy reserves are the amounts of money, including interest to be earned on the reserves, necessary to make up the difference between the net basic premium and the amounts needed to pay death benefits. If the expected mortality is lower than the mortality table figures or the interest earned is more than the policy requirements, the company has a surplus and a profit.

When you buy a level premium policy such as an ordinary (pay till you die or age 96) life, you agree to pay the same premium each year. In the earlier policy years you will pay a larger premium (advanced premium) than the policyholder's age warrants, and the extra premium is placed into a cash reserve. When the insurance laws were amended in the 1930's, a non-forfeiture (can't lose everything) law was passed that required the insurance companies to return part of the advance premiums in one of several different ways:

(1) If the policy is surrendered, there will be a cash refund (surrender value or cash value).

(2) The cash values can be used to buy a fully paid-up policy for a specified number of dollars, or the face value of the policy will be continued for a specified number of years. For example, a $1,000 ordinary life policy taken out at age 35 and held for 20 years has a cash value of $516, or will buy $583 worth of paid-up life insurance, or will continue the face value of $1,000 for 15 years and 318 days. Therefore, it might be profitable for you or your friends and relatives to investigate the possible value of "lapsed" and "worthless" policies. Some years ago, one of my clients had a "worthless" policy that had lapsed 4 years previously; the policyholder had died about 3½ years after the lapsing of the policy. The policy holder had paid premiums for 9 years, and I collected a large sum for the widow. The extended insurance feature had kept the policy in full force even though the family did not know it. They were going to throw the policy away as being worthless.

In all policies the cash reserve is much higher than the cash value or the surrender value. The life insurance companies say that, since the insured did not keep up his end of the contract and pay the premium for the entire life of the policy, they have the right to make a surrender charge. So they rebate the cash value and not the cash *reserve* value. Not many of the companies will tell you about this, and in fact most of the life insurance agents don't even know about it! Prove it to yourself. Ask your life insurance agent what the surrender charge in your policies is.

Another surrender charge is made if you take a paid-up policy instead of the cash. If you died within 1 year, even though they have "given" you a paid-up policy for 10 years, your beneficiaries will not get any refund of the paid-up premium. In fact, there is an interesting note at this point. This paid-up policy is actually a new term life insurance policy that the company is writing on you, usually without your knowledge. Often the life insurance agent that sold you the original policy doesn't even know it and most assuredly won't receive any commission on it.

You have heard insurance men say or have read advertisements to the effect that "You'll get every dollar spent in premium cost back and the policy will cost you nothing." This may be true for the cash premium outlay, but what of the interest cost? What would have been the difference if you had bought term insurance rather than a cash value policy and had invested the difference? Remember, at 5 percent per year, your money will double in 14½ years. Insurance men are fond of saying that insurance policies "force" people to save. The average life insurance policy is in force for 7 years. At the end of a 20-year period, one large life insurance company found that only 9 percent of all policies issued 20 years earlier were still in force or had been paid out in death claims!

On February 27, 1923, Roger Babson, one of the outstanding economists and financial advisors of America, made the following statement. "Let me repeat that I believe in life insurance. I wish that my clients would take out more. I simply urge that it be taken out as protection, the same as you would fire or auto insurance. But think twice before buying it as an investment. Those who have insurance to sell sometimes get over-enthusiastic and promise things which cannot be delivered. This is especially true when some life insurance agent attempts to sell life insurance as the best investment. With the greatest respect for the insurance companies, it could do no harm for such clients to obtain the advice of an impartial expert." To this, I can only say, Amen!

Present selling methods stress the most expensive forms of life insurance, which most policyholders cannot really afford. The primary purpose of protection has been distorted by selling agents who are out to get higher commissions. The enormous life insurance sales, which reach new records each year, indicate that the public wants and needs insurance protection. The large lapse rate of policies sold and not renewed is proof that the public is not getting protection they can afford or the type of protection they need.

I cannot recommend life insurance as an investment for anyone. For those who are ineligible to buy additional insurance because of illness, I recommend that they convert their policies into fully paid-up plans, or change them into lower-cost plans and start investing the difference in a true savings account.

I do recommend term life insurance as the basic and most necessary part of any financial plan.

MODERN FINANCIAL PLANNING

The past 5 years have seen the acceleration of the trend of insurance companies toward adopting the mutual fund industry. At one time, the life insurance industry was fighting mutual funds, but now they have seen that insurance plus mutual funds makes an ideal investment-protection package for most people. By the end of 1968, the figures of the National Association of Securities Dealers, Incorporated, showed that over 100 life insurance companies were now selling mutual funds. They either owned their own mutual funds or owned sales organizations that sold both funds and insurance. In 1969, over 25,000 life insurance salesmen were licensed to sell mutual funds, and it is estimated that in 1970 another 25,000 life insurance salesmen passed the qualification examinations to sell mutual funds.

Let us compare life insurance and equity investing, using the example of a man of 40 who has the choice of buying a $100,000 policy for a premium of $2,700 per year, or investing the $2,700 in an equity paying 8 percent per year. The insurance profit paid on death at age 45 would be $85,600, as compared to $14,600 in equity. In 15 years, at age 55, the insurance profit would be $46,000; that of the equity would be $54,000. At age 65 the insurance would show a loss of $12, while the equity would show a profit of $112,000.

Most modern financial plans have as their basis a combination of mutual funds for investment and life insurance for protection. Since these plans are primarily based on mutual fund investing, they are covered in Chapter 11.

LIFE INSURANCE ANNUITIES

An annuity is a contract generally sold by a life insurance company that will pay to the insured a specified amount of income for a specified period of time. Annuity payments are made up of a portion of the principal, plus interest, with the annuity return depending upon the life expectancy of the annuitant. An annuity is based upon the systematic liquidation of created and accumulated wealth. The safety of numbers is of the highest, since the company backing the annuity guarantees that the annuitant will not exhaust his capital before death. However, these fixed dollar annuities do involve the risk that inflation will reduce the buying power of the guaranteed income payments. Annuity proceeds are only partly taxable, as most of the payments can be considered a return of capital.

It is possible to put annuities in three major classifications:

(1) The Life Annuity provides the largest amount of income for a specified amount of capital. At the annuitant's death, the annuity contract terminates, with the company keeping any remaining value even though only a few payments may have been made.

(2) The 10 Years Certain and Life contract provides that monthly payments will be made for a minimum period of 10 years or for the life of the annuitant. A popular variation of this contract is the one whereby the company pays to the beneficiaries any difference between the purchase price of the annuity and the amount collected by the annuitant in monthly payments.

(3) The Joint and Survivor annuity makes a monthly income payment to two or more people as long as they may live. This form is generally the most popular for married couples.

Since women live longer than men, the amount of the monthly payment for a woman is smaller than that for a man. As an example of annuity payments, one of the largest life insurance companies has set up the following male rates for a $10,000 investment at a certain age:

Life annuity, $819 per year. Since this payout is only 8.2 percent per year, the insurance company will always profit on these annuities.

10 year certain, annual payments of $729.

15 year certain, annual payments of $729.

20 year certain, annual payments of $569.

As annuity payments vary between companies, it is best to shop around so as to get the highest payment possible. It is my recommendation that any investor should buy an annuity only to guarantee a certain number of dollars each month. To supplement these guaranteed dollars he should have a cushion of common stock, mutual funds, real estate income, or other equity investments that will compensate for the loss in the buying power of the annuity's guaranteed dollars.

An annuity's major investment value is peace of mind, not a high rate of return.

6

PENSION PLANS

Today we hear a lot about the "golden years" of retirement. Well, the best way to be old (if there is one) is to be financially independent. If you are old and have money, you are considered eccentric and are tolerated. If you're old and broke, you are considered crazy and are kept hidden. Actual figures show that only one person out of every three either can still earn his way or has enough money put aside for the retirement years.

In Chapter 3, we discussed Social Security retirement benefits. The Federal government figures that one-third of all Americans will be kept out of poverty by these Social Security benefits. These benefits should be the basis of your retirement program. Other benefits and retirement programs are added on so you may determine your future income.

Many people have life insurance policies that can be turned into a retirement plan as described in Chapter 5. In addition, many of us have GI insurance. Instead of cashing it in at age 65 for a lump sum, it is easy to request that the benefits be paid in monthly installments.

GOVERNMENT PENSION PLANS

The United States Civil Service Retirement System requires that eligible employees contribute 6.5 percent of their basic salary for pension and survivor benefits. They are guaranteed a return from the plan of at least the amount of their paid-in contributions, paid either to them or to their survivors. They must have worked under the system for at least 5 years, and they have to retire at age 70.

The amount of the retirement payment depends upon the length of service and the age at which the worker retires. The longer he works and the higher his salary, the more he will receive. His retirement benefit also varies depending upon whether he wants it to cover only himself or his survivors also.

If he selects an annuity without survivor benefits, when he dies the only payment made will be the difference between what he paid in and what he had received before death. If he selects an annuity with survivor benefits, his survivors can draw an annuity that is 55 percent of his basic annuity.

In addition to the regular contributions, he is allowed to make additional voluntary contributions to the Retirement Fund which will earn 3 percent per year compounded annually. When he retires, this money will be used to increase his annuity. Since this interest rate is so low and is even behind inflation, it is just giving money away to make any additional voluntary contributions.

All employee retirement records are maintained by the employees' agency. If there are any questions on the retirement plan, they can check with the personnel office. If you are contemplating working for the government, the retirement system should be checked out to see what your future benefits may be.

The Railroad Retirement Act now covers over 1,500,000 persons in this country. It is a federal retirement plan, very similar to the Civil Service Retirement System. In general, the employees of all railroads engaged in interstate commerce, the Railway Express, the Pullman Company railroad association, and railway labor organizations are covered.

The minimum length of service is 10 years, and military service in wartime or when required to serve is also counted. Survivor's annuities are also allowed as under the Civil Service Retirement Act. For further information you can consult the personnel official at your place of employment.

The Keough Plan for Self-Employed People is the biggest break independent businessmen have been given in years. Large corporations and businesses were able to set up profit-sharing and pension plans that allowed costs to be deducted from earnings. In passing the Keough Bill, Congress finally recognized that the small entrepreneur had been discriminated against. The Keough Bill allows such self-employed persons as doctors, lawyers, salesmen, store owners, accountants, and other small businessmen to set up retirement plans with tax benefits.

In 1962, Congress adopted the Self-Employed Individuals Tax Retirement Act to assist self-employed persons in building up a retirement program giving them the same benefits as if they worked for a large corporation with a retirement program. The first rules were so restrictive that only 7,366 retirement plans were started. In 1968, Congress eased some of the rules and made these plans practicable, so that 101,630 plans were approved in 1968 by the Internal Revenue Service. Briefly described, they allow self-employed persons to put up to 10 percent of their incomes (or $2,500, whichever is less) into a retirement fund. One-half of this amount is subtracted from the taxpayer's gross income. But the biggest advantage is that the taxpayer does not have to pay any taxes on the earnings of money invested in the retirement plan.

To show you how this benefit works, suppose you had a gross income of $36,000. If you did not have a Keough Plan, your tax would be (for a couple) $10,340 plus $775 surtax, or $11,115. If you had a Keough plan and invested the maximum of $2,500, your tax would be paid on $36,000 minus $2,500, or $33,500. The tax would be $9,988 or a tax savings of $1,127. Therefore, your Keough plan would cost you $2,500 minus $1,127, or $1,373 for a $2,500 investment.

There are a few limitations: you cannot start drawing it out until you are 59½ and you *must* start drawing it by 70½. If you need money and cancel out the plan before retirement age, there is a tax penalty. It must be understood this is a method of legally using a tax advantage. It does not mean that you will pay no taxes on this money. You will pay them later, but probably at a lower rate, since your income will be less when you retire. Another restriction is that you must provide for any full-time employees on the same percentage basis as your own participation. I recommend that every self-employed person have a Keough Plan.

You may invest your money in a mutual fund (the most popular), a bank savings account, Federal E or H bonds, savings and loan shares, etc. You should consult with your tax accountant, your attorney, and/or your stock broker.

PRIVATE PENSION PLANS

Private pension plans are becoming more and more popular as the average working man realizes that retirement is one of life's inevitables, unless he dies. Most people today realize that to retire on social security alone, without any additional income, is to retire to a bare subsistence.

If a company qualifies a retirement plan with the Internal Revenue Service, there are many tax advantages. A pension plan is a program to which your employer makes a contribution, counted by him as a business expense. Usually the contribution by the employer is a fixed percentage of his payroll or a specified amount each month for each employee. Employees are allowed to make a voluntary contribution to the plan up to a maximum of 10 percent of their compensation.

All earnings of the retirement plan are tax-free. The employee will be taxed on any profits received by him after he retires. If he takes his benefits in a lump sun, he will pay a capital gains tax. If he takes a monthly benefit, he will pay ordinary tax on the income he receives after he has recovered all of his contributions. As his income will probably be smaller, the tax incurred will be smaller also. Employees must realize that most of these private plans will return the amount deposited by the employee, but he will lose any contributions paid by the employer if he quits before retirement age. If your company does not have a retirement plan, why not ask a company official about it?

Private profit-sharing retirement plans are very similar in operation to private pension plans. The qualification of a profit-sharing plan with the Internal Revenue Service allows the company profits contributed to the plan to be deducted as a business expense. Most small companies will contribute a lump sum or a percentage of their profits, but they cannot contribute more than 15 percent of the wage of covered employees.

The money placed in both types of plans is handled by a trustee. The trustee will invest the money in a manner consistent with the investment objectives of the plan and the philosophy of the trustee and the employer. The money in the plan may be invested in either debt or equity securities or a mixture of the two.

Distributions from both types of plans may be made by a lump sum payment, installments for a fixed period of years, or a variable amount to be paid as long as funds are available. It is possible for each participant to have a co-beneficiary to help provide for a widow. In the profit-sharing plan, an employee can lose all claim to any benefits if he quits. Some plans allow the employee's accrued benefits to become "vested" over a period of time. Vested means that he does not lose the benefits if he quits, retires early, or is disabled or fired. Some plans will pay the vested amounts credited to an employee at the time he terminates his employment; others will keep it until retirement age.

The employer is able to judge exactly what his cost will be. The employee cannot judge what he will receive from the plan, however, because the rate of return of the investments and any capital gains will determine the amount in the plan that can be distributed.

Both retirement and profit-sharing plans are set up by employers to encourage their employees to make a career out of working for the company and to instill a sense of participation in the company's welfare. Profit-sharing plans are good only when the company makes money. And the easiest way for a company to make money is to have each employee take an active interest in the company's welfare.

7

YOUR OWN BUSINESS

One of the great American dreams is to have your name on the door and be the boss. There are millions of people who envy the self-employed business man because "he can do as he pleases." If you believe this, *then for your own sake* forget about going into business. Your attitude will doom your venture. The most demanding job in the world is the one where you are the boss and you own the business. You will find that the public tells you what hours to work. They'll give you orders for the goods or services they want. If you don't fill the needs of your customers, your competition will. The most successful businessman is the one who offers good, fast service and quality merchandise.

In 1968, over 450,000 new businesses were started, about 100,000 more than in 1962. Somewhere between 5 and 10 percent of these new businesses were franchise operations, including a great many food outlets. There are more people in business today in the United States than at any time in our history. Our Federal Government has been encouraging minority groups to go into business. A U.S. Government agency, the Small Business Administration, has been giving advice, furnishing operating ideas, and providing loans. Dun & Bradstreet, the largest business credit rating company and publisher of financial information, states that one half of new businesses will survive for 18 months, and that after a period of 10 years only 20 percent will still be in business.

This rate of failure is very high, and it is a tribute to American independence that people still try to create their own jobs and jobs for others.

It has been a constant amazement to me how people will, without adequate knowledge or training, put their life savings into a business venture, and even talk their relative and friends into doing the same. Lack of business knowledge causes most failures. Each person operating his own business, whether it is selling an intangible like sales advice, a service such as home cleaning or bookkeeping, or material items such as furniture or groceries, must know his business.

He must know how much initial capital is required to open his door for business. He must know what his requirements for merchandise will be, what store or office space, equipment, and labor he will need, how much overhead such as insurance and lights, fixtures, taxes, and deposits he must reckon with. He must be able to budget his continuing expenses such as rent, repairs, capital costs (interest), new merchandise, etc. He must be able to budget his cash flow—income versus cash spent for expenses. He must be prepared to lose money while he is getting established. And he must take the necessary steps such as advertising, promotions, or offering free services or advice to sell himself and his business to the buying public.

We have had several years of high income and prosperity, so there is a large reservoir of private savings available for investment as the necessary risk capital. The formation of new businesses will continue as long as our prosperity continues. A recession or depression causes a contraction of the amount of money in circulation. This drives up interest rates, thus lessening customer loans. To sell their merchandise, businesses will start price cutting, and profits will shrink. At this time there will be more business failures and a definite fall in the number of new business ventures launched.

REASONS FOR STARTING BUSINESSES

One of the major reasons for starting a new business venture is the desire for self-fulfillment. This motivating factor accounts for

20 percent of business starts, according to a recent survey. Most of the people with this as their driving force are out to prove something either to themselves or to someone else. While this motivating factor has led to some of the greatest successes in business, it cannot sustain most people over a long period of time. The rate of failure is much higher than among those who go into business for other reasons.

In an interview printed recently in a financial journal, the general partner and driving force in a small year-old business was quoted as saying he wanted a business dedicated to quality instead of "mass" appeal. He wanted a business that had a quality clientele to match the business. He wanted to know that he was right rather than to succeed by not being "true" to himself. His whole attitude was based on what he wanted and not on what his customers wanted or needed. His business is headed for failure unless he is fortunate enough to have some special dramatic flair, a special appeal, or an unusually loyal clientele and enough time and money to educate them. It was no surprise to me to read at the very end of the article that "he was looking for additional financial backing." He will probably contact his relatives and friends as the best available source of additional money. The tragic part of the entire affair is that, while being true to himself, he will financially destroy those who have the faith in him to put up additional capital for a doomed business.

The other major reason individuals seek self-employment is that they have the possibility of making more money than they do at their present jobs. There is a higher percentage of success when money is the motivating force. It is an easy motive to sustain and keeps on increasing as the self-employed's standard of living improves and requires additional income.

A special self-employed business category is the professional whose stock in trade is his time and knowledge. These include architects, attorneys, dentists, doctors, etc. These professionals have most of the problems of other businessmen, plus a few others. For example, doctors are not supposed to advertise but depend on word-of-mouth referrals. The decision to enter business generally depends upon professional contacts who will give referrals and organizations that furnish assistance. Many banks will finance necessary office costs and equipment needed by professionals, to be paid off in monthly payments as they get established. Banks offer them other assistance such as office location recommendations, equipment sources, and referrals.

Small service businesses have the greatest chance of success when the businessman is selling himself, his knowledge, and his willingness to serve his client's needs. In this area he has no competition. How many times each week do you look for some dependable, prompt, efficient, and reasonably priced service to solve some problem? As consumers we have a need that large companies cannot solve because of costs or inefficiency. If you as an investor can find a consumer need and fill it at a profit to yourself, then you can own a successful business overnight.

After you have been in business a short while, you'll make a disturbing discovery. People's tastes, wants, and needs keep changing. You must keep up with these changes; you can only run a profitable business with up-to-date answers for your clients. You must study the changing factors that affect you and your business. Some of the changes are in basic knowledge, additional new knowledge, customer desires and needs, competition, business methods, advertising, and government rules and regulations. If you are too far out in front you'll either go broke or become a millionaire. The old saying, "Build a better mousetrap and the world will beat a path to your door," is a lot of bunk. You must tell the world and then *sell* it your better mousetrap. Only if people believe you can you achieve success and prosperity.

YOU AND UNCLE SAM

Many people going into business for themselves forget that they take in a partner even before they open the doors. You may not want him but you will have him. His name is Uncle Sam. The Internal Revenue Service will take more than half your profits if you are very successful. But don't forget the family. There is Aunt Grabby from the state; and then there are Brother City, Sister County, and Cousin Special Agency. Regardless of how much you have in the till or the bank account, you had better have their share first. They'll want your money for income taxes, sales taxes, withholding taxes, property taxes, inventory taxes, permit taxes (commonly disguised as fees or service charges), special business taxes, and overriding taxes or assessments.

However, you as a businessman have one consolation if you are successful. You won't pay one cent of taxes yourself! When you figure your overall costs for your services or merchandise, you'll consider taxes as part of your costs. You'll collect taxes from your customers and then pass them on to the government. Taxes and their record-keeping are a big cost of doing business. The main variable in tax accounting is the percentage of tax and the cost of keeping track of it, which will depend upon your sales volume.

REQUIREMENTS FOR SUCCESS

The main requirement for going into business is knowledge: of management, business methods, competition, customers, government regulations, taxes, sources of information or goods—all of which can be summed up as "knowledge of your business." However, most people overlook another form of required knowledge. This is knowledge of yourself. How will you react to various problems? Do you like people and do you get along with them? Do you trust your clients and do they trust you? Do you feel that you have done your clients a favor and helped them when you have made a sale? Or do you feel that you have taken advantage of them and this is the last time you'll ever see them? Do you take an interest and can you solve your client's problems? Are you willing to listen and can you accept advice from your clients, your friends, and/or your competition? Are you willing to incur a loss to correct a mistake you have made? If you can't honestly answer these questions affirmatively, then don't go into business.

Business failures can be attributed to a lack of willingness to learn your business, will to succeed, or ability to manage yourself and the business. To have a successful business, you must be happy in the work, enjoy being identified with it, be proud to offer its products or services; and you must become emotionally adjusted to that particular line of endeavor. You must be a positive, happy, friendly, and constructive person, for the world loves success and an honest smile. The world shies away from complainers, liars, cheats, and thieves. A successful businessman is a success in his family and civic life as well as his business life. Self-employment is not an escape from authority or responsibility to yourself. Observe other businessmen. Can you do better than they? Ask those who you do business with about your chances as a businessman. But most of all, consider what the effect will be on your wife and family.

If your wife is absolutely against it, my advice is to forget self-employment. A successful business can only be built when there is family harmony and cooperations. A friend of mine bought a restaurant franchise. At the end of the first year, he had increased his income from $7,000 to $22,000. He had worked an average of 102 hours a week (up from 40) and had separated from his family. His marriage was breaking up because he put business first.

He would not pay this price, so he sold the franchise at a slight loss. He now makes $9,000 a year, works regular hours, and has reconciled with his wife. He has a happy home life again and in my opinion is a more successful man. To work for yourself you must work harder and longer hours, and you must consider this as a price to be paid.

SELECTING YOUR BUSINESS

In choosing a business, I suggest you stick to a field you know. Enroll in any courses that could be of help, such as those given by a junior college or trade institute. Many of these courses can be taken at night or at home by correspondence. First-hand observation or working experience in a proposed business (such as a working apprenticeship of a few months or so) can help you avoid many pitfalls. Many trade associations or professional societies offer specialized training. Ask a successful man in the business you have chosen for advice, for successful people are generally nice people and willing to help others.

Sources of printed material include the Small Business Administration, which has offices in most major cities. Local trade groups such as a chamber of commerce can be of great help. There are many national associations and societies with abundant literature. Often overlooked are the facilities of a full service commercial bank; these can furnish many services such as surveys of business activities in your area. These surveys cover population, number and types of businesses, area growth, taxes, money flow, proposed new developments, consumer habits, etc. The new or small businessman may find that his best financial friend will be his bank. Libraries and commercial bookstores have general and sometimes specific information about many types of businesses. Check your phone book or a business directory in your town or the nearest large city for trade groups who might send you information. Professional people spend years in college training, so don't rush out and invest in a business without proper preparation.

There are many businesses you should not consider because of competition. For example, it would be foolish to open up a "Mom and Pop" grocery store across the street from a supermarket. If you did make a success of it by staying open longer hours or selling items they didn't have, you would find that as professional businessmen they would meet your "competition" very quickly, and their greater resources, including both money and personnel, would eventually beat you.

FRANCHISING

Franchising is a means of going into business for yourself in cooperation with a management company. It offers the franchise company (franchisor) the opportunity to acquire good workers (the investors), additional capital, and a method of fast company expansion.

The 1968 sales volume of franchised business within the United States was over $89 billion, which was an increase of $9 billion or 11 percent over 1967. One of the pioneering companies in this field was the Gamble Skogmo Company, which had a 1968 sales volume of $400 million. It is possible to buy a franchise for an employment agency or a bookkeeping and tax service; you can sell hot dogs or hamburgers or run a night club; shine shoes by machines or sell house cleaning services or weight-watching club memberships.

The major advantage to the investor in buying a franchise operation is that he becomes part of an organized operation run by experienced management that provides him with advice and knowledge. This should enable the investor to by-pass the initial trial and error period that causes so many go-it-alone entrepreneurs to go into bankruptcy.

The second major benefit to the investor is the public recognition of a quality franchise and the services it may expect. For example, when you see the "Golden Arches" of the MacDonald's Hamburger shops you know, through advertising or having been a customer, that the food and service will be the same as in the outlet in your home town. A recognized quality franchise outlet is a place of buying confidence. It is a welcome and recognized friend when you are a traveler in a strange town. However, it also works in reverse. I went into an auto repair service franchise and got stuck for a bill that was over $100, or four times the advertised rate for a brake reline. So there is one franchise I won't recommend or patronize again.

The initial capital required varies from a few hundred dollars for a string of postage dispensing machines to hundreds of thousands for an auto accessories business. Most franchises seem to require an initial investment of from $8,000 to $20,000. Then they generally have an additional management fee which is a percentage of your gross sales. Most of the franchises in the food or merchandise lines also require that you purchase only their products, which can be either a blessing or highly expensive.

Your profit potential varies greatly. For example, an Orange Julius soft drink stand has a very small profit on each item, so your income and total profit are dependent upon a high volume of sales. On some of the management or sales courses that are sold through franchises, the profit is several hundred dollars per sale, so the sales volume can be much lower and still show a handsome profit. If the total number of sales is high, then with a large profit per sale you would have a higher potential for profit.

Like most other investments, franchises have several special and unique problems that you must solve before buying one. You must select a franchise investment with care and only after a thorough investigation, as you will be entering into a long-term business marriage. Mistakes are costly in both peace of mind and money. The following list of eleven questions will give you some idea of what to look for in a franchise, how to evaluate one, how to compare it with other investments including similar franchises, and what to expect. As you go through these questions remember (if you intend to invest in one) that you are going to represent the franchise, be an active worker, and be identified with it. You must be willing to accept in full, and I stress the word *full,* the philosophies, procedures, and ideas of your franchising group or you will be unhappy and you won't realize the full benefits offered. This could cause you to become a failure. If you answer any of these questions negatively, you should invest your money in a different franchise company.

(1) Are there successful operating franchises making money now?

(2) Are you encouraged to talk to present franchise owners?

(3) Are you advised to check with your own attorney, accountant, or advisors? (If you are being rushed into buying, *look out!*)

(4) Are you required to qualify for a franchise according to your moral background, business experience, education, reputation, etc? (If your financial status is the only qualification, it means they are interested only in your money and not in your success.)

(5) Does the franchisor offer you constant supervision, guidance, promotional aids, advertising, accounting, purchasing, and other management and merchandising advice and services?

(6) Do they offer you a comprehensive training course?

(7) Do they offer a recruiting and training course for employees you may need?

(8) Does the franchisor provide you with references and financial statements for you to check with your banker, etc?

(9) Will they give you copies of all contracts to be signed and all guarantees so you may take them to your attorney or banker?

(10) Will they furnish you with a survey or justification for the selection of your franchise site showing financial projections, size of market, competition, etc?

(11) Do they have a plan for continuous growth and expansion of the entire franchise program?

Yes answers to the above questions point out some advantages of franchise operations that can solve many of the ordinary problems faced by businessmen everywhere.

To evaluate this type of investment properly, I suggest you talk to present franchise owners and not just accept sales brochure testimonials. You must remember that present franchise owners will have a tendency to put their franchise in the best possible light so as to show strangers they did not make a bad investment. You should make inquiries with the Better Business Bureau; with your banker about the financial stability of the franchisor; visit with possible competitors or those operating similar franchises. You should compare operating costs and profit potential with owners of similar businesses. Investigate as thoroughly as you can and take your time. Do not be rushed into an investment, especially by the line that all of the franchises will be sold and you'll miss out. Remember that haste and greed can blind an investor into making a profitless investment.

If you are interested in a franchise operation, you should subscribe to *Modern Franchising* magazine, 1033 First Ave., Des Plaines, Illinois 60016. It is full of advertisements and testimonials which should be read with caution. Many excellent articles, operating ideas, and good advice make it one of the best sources of information for you.

A FORMULA FOR FRANCHISE PROFITS

Many times I have found in talking to franchise owners that they have not properly evaluated the rate of return on their investment or cannot calculate their profit. Many franchise owners find that they have bought themselves a job—a low-pay, long-hours job with very limited profit potential. The following formula will quickly enable you to make a preliminary estimate so that you won't waste time on unnecessary negotiations, investigations, or site selections.

First, multiply the initial investment required to buy the franchise by 8 percent. That figure, 8 percent, is the amount of profit you could reasonably expect to make with the same money in another investment. For example, $20,000 times 8 percent is $1,600 per year. Then find the rate of pay for working as a manager in the franchise's industry on an annual basis for the number of hours you will be required to work. If the pay is $150 per week for 40 hours and you must put in 60 hours of work, use a pay scale of $225 per week (disregarding premium pay for overtime) or $11,700 per year. $11,700 plus $1,600 is $13,300. If your franchise won't net you (before taxes) an additional 50 percent or $6,650 for a total of $19,950 per year, forget it. You must be paid for your investment, your job time, and the management responsibilities you must assume. I have used 50 percent as a pay factor for your management responsibility. You must be paid your actual worth. I have used 8 percent of the original outlay because it is easy to find long-term investments that will return 8 percent per year without effort or time on your part, such as raw land, mutual funds, or common stocks.

I have observed that franchise operations generally need the owner's physical presence to secure maximum efficiency and profit. Personal interest and operation by the owner are the personal sacrifice that owning your own business requires. Most of the failures in this field can be directly attributed to lack of interest, unwillingness to learn, not following the franchisor's guidelines, and not working hard enough.

Franchising is recommended for persons who are going into business for the first time, or for those who have sufficient capital to invest in a full-time business that requires management skills the investor does not have. It is also recommended for highly competitive businesses such as restaurants, high-volume food outlets, and other retail outlets with constantly changing business circumstances or problems.

Franchising is not recommended for non-technical or easily imitated businesses or services such as house cleaning or fast print shops. If the business is low volume or high inventory, or if low-priced items constitute the main business, as in a hardware store, drug store, or gift shop, it is my opinion they should be avoided unless there are especially profitable factors peculiar to that individual franchise outlet (such as location).

8

REAL ESTATE

Real estate is the oldest form of property. Land was created before man and sustains him, and man seems to have an inherent desire to own his own land and build on it. Most people consider land the most desirable form of security. They can walk on it, feel it, and build on it.

But a home should not be bought with the expectation that it will return a profit as a monetary investment. When all of the costs are carefully computed—depreciation, taxes, maintenance, and loss of interest on the capital you have in the house—you may find that home ownership is not profitable. But when you consider that owning your home has a social value, that it gives a tremendous satisfaction, then it is a good property to have on an economic basis. It often provides a better and more gracious living atmosphere than a rented home.

In large cities, property taxes have risen enormously in the past few years. Home owners throughout the United States pay property taxes far out of proportion to the tax structure. In smaller cities and rural areas, homes historically have retained their market prices better than most other forms of property.

One of the unrecognized benefits of a fully paid-up home for older persons is that it provides lower rent (in taxes and upkeep), which is another way of saying more income. When buying a house it is my recommendation that you buy a decreasing term life insurance policy to cover the mortgage. No widow should be forced to worry about making house payments.

The supply of real estate is limited and will become more so. Future growth of our population, with its need for goods and services, means that cities will grow larger and more land will be put into productive use. More population means that farms must produce more. The population of the United States is expected to grow by 1985 to 300 million people. This 50 percent increase in the number of people living in the U.S. will drive real estate values up.

Homes have been growing in value by about 5 percent per year over the past few years. When the home-owner sells and makes a nice profit, he will find that the price of a new house to replace the one that he just sold will have risen in proportion. To avoid income tax on any "profit," the seller must buy a new house of the same price or higher.

REAL ESTATE INVESTMENT PROBLEMS

City land values have been rising for many years, and it is most unlikely that these values could be wiped out. Real estate investing cannot be done on a long-term 100-year basis. Real estate values must rise during the time the investor owns it. Business conditions, economic trends, and neighborhood planning all contribute to the value of real estate. Following are some of the problems that real estate investors must solve in order to profit:

(1) Real estate lacks ready marketability. Buyers must be found and titles guaranteed. The investor must be able to wait out any selling time required.

(2) Real estate generally is one of the last investments to rise in inflation. Wages, taxes, and other costs go up faster than rent or sales price.

(3) Real estate is very sensitive to local property conditions. Some areas are booming, such as Southern California, while South Dakota is losing population. The same boom-bust can occur in various sections of the same city. Maintenance costs are high, and since they are mostly based on labor, they are destined to go higher.

(4) Real estate is poor collateral if money is needed in a hurry. The time involved for appraisals, title searches, and arranging a loan can take the best part of a month.

(5) Real estate taxes are rising and will continue to do so.

BENEFITS

Some of the benefits of owning real estate are the following:

(1) Well-selected real estate more often than not is one of the best long-term investments, due to inflation and population needs.

(2) Real estate provides a large leverage factor, as the down payment is usually under 30 percent. Thus you can have borrowed money working for you. As inflation cuts the buying power of the dollar, mortgages on real estate will be paid off in cheaper dollars; thus a high mortgage payment today might be a much smaller one in relation to the investor's future income.

(3) Real estate is good collateral for long-term loans if one is not pushed for time.

FIX-IT-UP PROJECTS

For the average investor who is short on money but is handy with tools and has sufficient time, the repairing of houses for resale or rent can prove to be extremely profitable. Because of the high cost of hiring plumbers, carpenters, and other construction workers, older house are often demolished instead of being repaired and brought up to modern building standards. Many times repairable property can be bought for land costs only. The cost of the place plus required materials should not total more than 75 percent of the current market value of a similar property. The 25 percent balance should be considered as payment for the time the investor has put into the place.

Investors who cannot do the work themselves must be able to estimate the construction materials needed and the amount and cost of labor accurately. They should also have the knowledge to handle the legal details, collect rents, supervise maintenance, and be their own architects and building contractors. If you can't do some of the work, you should not consider this form of investing. You must consider that your time is part of the raw materials that add to the cost of repairing the property.

RENTAL PROPERTY

Buying a piece of rental property with a small down payment and paying it off through rent receipts can be quite a gamble. Some of the cost figures, such as mortgage payments, remain fairly stable, while others such as maintenance, taxes, and building materials, have undergone tremendous inflation. Most investors do not consider the hidden costs that could wipe them out. Some of these costs are vacancies, building code upgrading, and such community improvements as sewer or street assessments. I believe that landlords should allow a reasonable percentage deduction from estimated income for vacancies, based upon the locality. Investors must know whether the area is dependent upon one or two industries and how stable they are. For example, in the Cape Kennedy area in Florida, property prices have declined due to the slow-down in space shots. This will leave the area over-built for a few years until population growth can fill in for the space industry. New apartments can cause perfectly good older apartments to suffer a loss of tenants if the rents are more reasonable or they have such luxuries as a swimming pool. Apartment houses should return 10 percent or more in net profits before taxes.

FARMS

Many investors buy farms for tax advantages and not in order to farm for profit. Today there are about 3 million farms in the U.S., only half of the number 30 years ago. One-third of all farms are classified as commercial, grossing over $10,000 per year. Another one-third are those that gross less than $10,000 per year; the rest are residential farms. Many investors have purchased farms to use as a commercial venture, intending to offset farm losses against profits from other businesses, investments, or salaries. They count on depreciation and the rising prices of farm lands to make a profit over a long period.

Farms are growing larger and more mechanized. They are becoming more of a big business. There has been a great outcry against federal subsidies to farms. As more people have moved to the cities, the political power of farmers has gone down. Since many farm investments depend upon depreciation, loopholes in the tax laws, and federal subsidies, this type of investing is becoming more hazardous.

If you are contemplating an investment in farm land as a method of beating income taxes, you are treading on dangerous ground. If the tax laws change, you could suffer a large capital loss. Farm investing should be undertaken only by very knowledgeable people who are willing to undergo rural living and long hours of hard labor. It is just a question of time until Congress cuts farm subsidies or even eliminates them.

UNIMPROVED PROPERTY

A bigger profit per dollar can be made in unimproved property than in other forms of real estate investing. You have several important points to consider before buying. You must know the economic progress of the area where the land is located. If it is a good growth area, the projected population should double (or more) every 5 years. The profitability of a piece of unimproved land will depend mainly on the amount of the down payment plus the total payments while owning the land, and on the length of time the investor holds it.

Most unimproved land provides no income unless it is used for farming. The investor must carry all costs out of his current income and should consider them an additional cash investment in the property. Land can be considered as going through development cycles. First, it will be raw land with nothing on it. There will be no interest in it, as it is not located in a developed or developing area. As nearby areas are developed, land investors will begin to appreciate the opportunities of outlying properties. Until this time, the land has been valued as bare or agricultural property. As more investor interest is shown in the predevelopment state, the locality's property prices will begin to rise and then will reach a point at which it is not profitable to buy the land for farming. It is still too early for urban use such as industrial sites, residential developments, or commercial and institutional complexes. The third stage comes when the land is actually developed.

The greatest profit potential is found when the land is in the predevelopment stage. A good raw land investment should return 25 percent per year for the time held. Generally, it takes from 3 to 8 years for land to go from the undeveloped stage into the predeveloped stage.

RECREATION LAND

This is raw land near a lake, river, or seaside, or in the mountains. Its main development comes from vacation homes, recreation parks, or retirement living. For the past 5 years this type of land has been appreciating at an annual rate of more than 18 percent per year. With more leisure time on their hands, Americans have been enjoying vacations and extended trips and buying vacation retreats.

Many investors have purchased land expecting that even if they paid a little too much this year, inflation will cause the property to be worth more than they paid for it in a year or so; so why worry? This inflationary state of mind also contributes to rising prices.

There are tax advantages in buying real estate for investment purposes. Real estate investors can depreciate their investment over a period of years, because buildings are expected to deteriorate with time. This depreciation is a paper write-off, and in fact the value of the building may be going up. If depreciation plus mortgage interest and maintenance is more than the property income, the investor can take this loss and balance it against current income from other sources such as rent, salary, dividends, etc.

When the property is sold the investor pays a capital gains tax on the difference between the value of the depreciated property and the sales price. For example, an apartment purchased for $100,000 may be held for 10 years, depreciated $5,000 per year, and then sold for $140,000. The capital gains tax would be paid on $40,000 plus $50,000 depreciation, or $90,000 at a tax rate of 25 percent. Since income taxes go to 70 percent, you can see that a 25 percent income tax rate is a real savings.

REAL ESTATE MUTUAL FUNDS

Here is a new form of real estate investment. The funds will specialize in short-term construction and development loans. The rate on these loans is much higher than on conventional long-term mortgage loans, and they run from 6 to 24 months in length.

Some of the problems to be considered by the fund's management include questions such as "Can the building be completed on time?" "Can costs be kept within the budget?" and "Will permanent financing be available in a future money market?"

These funds intend to comply with the Internal Revenue Code and pass 90 percent or more of the fund's net profits on to the shareholders so as to operate income tax free.

Loans to be made will include the "wrap-around loan." This type of loan is made in addition to any existing mortgages. Since they are not as safe as a first mortgage, they usually carry a higher interest rate. Short-term warehousing loans to mortgage banking companies will be made using their first mortgages as collateral. Gap loans are those that fill the time interval between the construction loan and the permanent financing arranged after the building has reached a satisfactory occupancy rate. These loans are made on commercial and apartment buildings.

If the operators of the fund are well-qualified, they will be able to manage themselves any property they may have to foreclose on or buy as distressed property. This will allow them to rehabilitate the property, operate it, or resell it.

Real estate funding is a leverage technique and is sometimes used in real estate investing in the following manner: The investor puts a lump sum into a real estate syndicate, say $25,000. The real estate syndicate will have an income yield of perhaps 10 percent. This income is then invested in mutual fund shares and a small part in decreasing term insurance. These speculative techniques can be profitably used by investors who have the ability to absorb losses without letting it bother them too much. This kind of speculation is recommended for persons in the higher income tax brackets or for single persons who are willing to wait some time to cash in any realized profits. You should go into this only if you are sure that the management of the real estate syndicate is competent and experienced.

MORTGAGES

Mortgages are contracts that give the lender a lien on a piece of real property. They receive a specified rate of interest over the length of the loan. In 1967, the average first mortgage rate was 6.75 percent. In 1970, the rate had risen to 7.9 percent. Many home mortgages are backed by the federal government and are called FHA loans. Mortgages issued by banks and savings and loan companies charge higher rates than the FHA rate.

Many investors will buy second or third mortgages. These loans are subject to the mortgage that precedes them. If a first mortgage is foreclosed, the holder of the second mortgage must pay off the first mortgage or lose his investment. Most mortgages are for long periods of time, and inflation has caused mortgage investors to lose money. Mortgage loans are made for small sums as well as for sums running into the millions. Investors needing cash find that sometimes it is difficult and expensive to sell the mortgage to other investors.

REAL ESTATE SYNDICATIONS

This method of real estate investing is promoted by a general partner who, for the real estate fees, sales fee, and maintenance fees, manages the property. Participation units of $2,500 or more are sold to investors (limited partners). Anticipated income comes from depreciation and should be estimated at 8 percent or more. Income from depreciation is a return of capital and is tax free. Property is sold after 7 years when depreciation is low and the investor receives a taxable capital gains. Many syndications show losses that can be credited against other income for the first few years. If Congress changes the depreciation laws downward, syndication investing will suffer. It's an excellent investment for long-term investors, high income investors, and those who can hold the investment, as there is a limited resale market.

9

THE STOCK MARKET

It is impossible to cover stock market investing in detail in one chapter. There have been thousands of books written on this subject. But I have found that most books are full of technical details or use a vocabulary that is really Greek to the average investor, and so are worthless to him. The most popular books have been those that pushed a "guaranteed-never-lose system of beating the market" or told you how to "make a million easily without risk." This is impossible.

This chapter will cover just a few basic stock market pointers that are generally overlooked. It also has some investment ideas and suggestions on what to look for and how to buy and sell.

"Stock market" is a broad term that refers to all the processes of investing in stocks, bonds, commodities, and mutual funds. It is not a single thing, and the stock market does not move as a block. Some stocks will go up when the market is going down and vice versa, so there is always a market within the market.

Several indexes are used to measure the stock market's performance, such as the popular Dow Jones averages. Another index that uses a greater number of companies in its calculations is the Standard and Poor index, which has shown over the past 10 years an annual average rise of 7.8 percent.

About 76 percent of the total volume of stocks traded on the exchanges are traded on the New York Stock Exchange. The balance are traded on the American Stock Exchange and the various regional exchanges scattered throughout the United States. The exchanges establish trading rules and furnish the facilities for trading. They do not buy or sell or make a market for any shares. The trading of stocks is done by the exchange members for their customers or for their own trading accounts.

UNRECOGNIZED INFLUENCES ON THE MARKET

Some of the major factors affecting stock market prices, outside of technical and economic ones, are not generally noticed.

One of the strong stock market price influencers is the percentage of cash that large institutional accounts have on hand. In February, 1969, the banks, life insurance companies, pension plans, and mutual funds had over $5 billion in cash. Since mutual funds cannot show any performance records with cash or debt investments, this large supply of money must eventually be invested. In 1968, institutions had almost $10 billion to invest in the stock market. It was estimated that only $4 billion in new shares was created through new stock issues. This meant that there was an additional $6 billion of demand for a shrinking number of shares. This is one of the reasons that I believe there will not be any big or lasting stock market slump. Institutions now account for about 60 percent of all stock market exchange trading, and they cannot hold cash for too long. Since the supply of good, growth investment stock issues is getting smaller while the demand is growing, it is just a matter of time until pressure from institutional bidding forces stock prices upward.

In such periods as the first half of 1969, when stock market professionals, brokers, salesmen, analysts, and advisors were at odds with each other about the market's direction, investors tend to become very selective. Many issues will resist downside pressure; they will still decline, but not as much as the general market. Stocks of weak, poorly managed companies or those with serious problems become very vulnerable and drop much faster than the stock market indexes. As it becomes harder and harder for the experts and professionals to find stocks that are reasonably good investments, they become nervous and, as smart money managers, sell at the first sign of weakness in any company. It is my belief that half of any stock price is based on emotions. The other half is based on fundamentals such as earning power.

If you are looking for an undervalued investment or a bargain, you must look for stocks that have been overlooked, are not popular, or have a bad name. When most of the investment analysts favor a certain stock, you will find that it is no longer a bargain. It might be an excellent investment, but the results are not going to be very spectacular. If a security is a favorite you will find that it is fully valued. Those who recognized the basic value in the stock early will make the largest profits for being alert enough to see the investment opportunity. If a stock is out of favor, unrecognized, or in an unpopular industry, it will take careful investigation to determine what, if any, basic value it has and the probable market reaction.

There is an investment theory of "contrary opinion" that works on the assumption that the general public is always late and wrong. They believe that most investors or traders buy when the smart money professionals are selling and sell when the market is off. The investors who follow this theory need a lot of courage to act against public opinion, market behavior, and the popular investment psychology of the times.

Many investors buy stocks because of an emotional attraction. They may have worked for the issuing company, inherited the stock from a loved one, or felt that the stock has been good to them. They may just want to be able to say, "I'm in the market. . . . I've got some IBM," but this is actually an investment for the ego. You must remember that the only reason you are buying a stock and holding it is to make money, not to own stock for stock's sake. Stocks are and must be viewed as a way for you to accumulate wealth.

STOCK BROKERS

Investing is a service business. All stock brokers offer you their knowledge, experience, contacts, information, and facilities. You are dependent upon their integrity, knowledge, ethics, and dedication to their business. A stock broker's main asset is himself, and the next most important thing is personnel who are in the business of money management for you. These people must be able to make knowledgeable decisions when called upon to do so. They must balance the inherent risks of the investment under consideration against the probability of profit. Many investors will ask, "If this stock you're recommending to me is undervalued, why hasn't someone else bought it?" If the salesman cannot give good economic and background reasons for the purchase or cannot rely upon his source of information, the investment cannot be a good one.

If your broker is interested in developing a strong business relationship with you, then you can have faith in him. I suggest that you stick with your stock advisor through good and bad decisions and not switch advisors each time you get a loser. You can't make a profitable investment every time, but over the long term sensible investors will profit. A competent broker who is interested in you can be your best financial friend.

Any broker you deal with will be licensed by your state and registered with the Securities & Exchange Commission (SEC), and both he and his registered representative should be members of the National Association of Securities Dealers, Inc.

I was a stock investor long before I became a salesman and later a broker. A stock broker is the owner or partner of a brokerage house, and the salesmen are registered representatives who commonly call themselves brokers. It was my experience that I received more service and personal attention from small brokerage houses; I was very important to them. Small brokers must give personalized attention to their clients to compete with some of the services and financial reports that the large brokerage houses provide. Small brokers can get much of the same financial information but it takes longer. There has been a lot of publicity by New York Stock Exchange members telling you that they are better firms for you to deal with. In my opinion, you should deal with the broker who has a personal interest in you, your financial problems, and your efforts to solve them.

The biggest stock brokerage house, Merrill, Lynch, Pierce,

Fenner & Smith, without conceding any wrong-doing, accepted some SEC-imposed penalties in 1968 for allegedly passing inside information to 15 of its largest institutional customers. The SEC charged that the Merrill Lynch salesmen were selling Douglas Aircraft stock to the firm's ordinary customers, while the firm's executives were passing on information to the large institutional investors that Douglas profits were due for a sharp drop. While this is discrimination against the smaller individual client, it would be silly for any businessman not to attempt to take care of his largest, best, and most profitable accounts first. This is a natural reaction.

There have been a number of lawsuits filed against stock brokers who were officers or directors of publically held companies. These lawsuits often charge that the brokers have profited from inside information. As a result, many companies have lost the services of experienced and qualified financial advisors due to resignations of stock brokers from directorships and corporate positions. They feel that they cannot afford to be sued. Make no mistake about it, inside information is still being passed around. Insiders are still profiting from privileged information and will continue to do so.

I believe it is completely unethical for some brokerage company salesmen to call clients and say "Sell Ford," while others in the same company are telling their clients to buy Ford. If stock is recommended for trading by a brokerage, all of the men should be telling their clients the same story.

KINDS OF STOCKS

Listed stocks: the term applied to the stock issues that are qualified on the New York Stock Exchange and other exchanges. The companies listed on exchanges are generally the larger and more substantial corporations.

Over-the-counter stocks: those that are not traded on an exchange, but are bought and sold by negotiation through stock brokers. There is a National Quotation Service that sends out a listing each trading day showing what issues the stock brokers are willing to buy and sell and the trading price. About 30,000 different issues are listed daily. They include most of the banks and insurance companies, the smaller, newer corporation issues, mutual fund shares, and stocks of local appeal.

The third market: the term used to describe the trading of listed stocks in the over-the-counter market. Many brokers, especially the smaller ones, do not belong to stock exchanges, and they trade listed stocks between themselves for their clients. Many large stock trades are handled in this manner to cut commission costs, stock exchange fees, or state taxes.

Trading in tomorrow's commodities: The trading of contracts to buy or sell commodities such as eggs, live hogs, silver, or pork bellies at a future date is termed commodity trading.

Most commodities are in heavy supply at certain seasons of the year. If they were brought to market at this time, the prices realized would be very low. When the supply had dried up, the prices would rise sharply. Commodity trading was started primarily to level out price fluctuations by contracting to supply certain amounts at a specified time in the future. Commodity contracts call for the investor to either buy a contract to accept delivery or sell a contract to make delivery in the future. Commodity speculators seldom make or take a delivery, as they sell their contracts before the delivery date.

Besides speculators, who hope to profit by taking advantage of price changes, there are two major groups of commodity investors influencing prices. The first group consists of those who are engaged in the raising or handling of commodities (such as grain elevator operators). The other group includes the processors or manufacturers who use the commodities (such as General Foods Corporation, which produces flour and packaged cereals). The latter trade in commodities primarily to hedge on prices and to keep prices as even as possible so as to control their raw material costs and maintain merchandising stability. These investors have trained agricultural specialists who keep track of the amount of commodities that will be available—for instance, how much wheat was planted and what effect the weather has had. This enables them to predict the commodities market. The speculator must be very nimble and lucky to buck these knowledgeable investors and make a profit.

If you are blessed with iron nerve, are able to smile when you have taken a beating, and can afford to lose your entire investment, then you might consider commodity trading. If you would like to say to a friend, "I just bought 30,000 pounds of pork bellies and made $450 today," or you enjoy the thrill of a panic every day, then look into commodity trading.

Commodity mutual funds: In July, 1969, the Chicago Board of Trade (most commodities are traded in Chicago) announced regulations to govern trading in fund accounts. There have been several commodity funds operating for the past few years, but they have not been very popular. Commodity funds pay taxes like any other company and do not have the tax advantages of regular mutual funds. As most commodity contracts are for less than 6 months, most of the profits will be short-term profits subject to regular income taxes. This trading is recommended for knowledgeable speculators only. The Comsec Fund is the first Mutual Fund that can invest in commodities. They are limited to 10 percent of their total assets in commodities.

TECHNICAL FUNDAMENTALS

Many investors and professional analysts use technical fundamentals to chart and forecast the stock market. They use charts, graphs, etc. to show stock market prices, price changes, daily trading volume, corporate valuations, cash flow, and gross volume receipts. It is impossible to cover these in this book, and stock market investors will find that there are innumerable books on the Dow Jones Theory and technical aids. Your own stock broker can furnish you with most of the technical information you may need. Three technical tools in general use are described in the next three paragraphs.

Price-earnings ratio (PE): The ratio is the current market price, say $30, divided by the latest earnings, say $2 per year, to give the PE ratio of 15 to 1 ($15 invested for every $1 earned) times earnings. The Dow Jones industrial averages in recent years have ranged from a PE low of 8 to 1 to a high PE of 22 to 1.

Many investors feel that stable, mature companies' PE ratio should be 8 to 1 or less and growth companies' about 17 to 1. Many of the highly speculative hot stock issues have PE ratios of 40 or 60 to 1, or even more.

Stock market indexes: the most popular way to judge the market's direction and strength. The Dow Jones industrial average is composed of 60 stocks and is the most quoted index. The Standard and Poor index covers 500 New York Stock Exchange listings and is a broader measurement.

Dividend influences: The Dow Jones industrial dividend yield was at a low of 2.95 percent in 1965, and was as high as 6.85 percent in 1950. When the stock market as a whole rises, the dividend yield tends to go down. Growth companies pay low dividends, as they need to reinvest earnings for additional facilities to continue their growth. Mature companies tend to pay out most, usually about 65 percent, of their net earnings. Most other forms of investing, such as S & L accounts, banks, and bonds, have paid higher dividends since 1958. Stocks are recommended for growth, not income.

HOW TO BUY

Buying: one of the most important factors in stock market investing is knowing when to buy. The investor who waits for a favorable market will wait until he dies without finding it. At any given time, you will find some intelligent market professionals forecasting doom and others who can see nothing but silver-lined clouds. When all analysts agree, it's time to get scared or start using the contrary investing system.

The best time to invest is when you have the money. In buying shares you will find that sometimes the purchase price is different from the price published in the paper. These published prices don't show all of the trading. Published prices for over-the-counter (OTC) stocks show the wholesale price and do not include any mark-ups or commissions. If you really want to buy a particular stock, have your salesman offer a small advance of an eighth of a point more than the current market price. I seldom place an order at a round figure such as $20; instead I try a bid of

$20¼. If there are 20 buyers at $20, my higher bid will get me my investment immediately. Most brokers are very competitive and charge the New York Stock Exchange Commission scale for listed stocks and most OTC issues. Many times the OTC issues are traded on a principal basis out of the broker's inventory and he will add a commission figured in points.

Sometimes you profit more by not investing. If your main purpose in buying a stock is to unload it on some sucker at a later date for a higher price, don't buy it—you may find that you are the sucker. Every stock eventually establishes a market price based on earning power or asset value, and if these turn out to be zero the stock will be zero too!

Stay out of junk! You'll always be able to buy, but many times you will find there are no buyers when you want to sell. I know a doctor who bought 240,000 shares of a shell company at 40¢ per share. When the stock was pushed up to $3.25, he thought he'd sell out and make a fortune. He ended up selling 3,000 shares at 75¢ each and now has 237,000 pieces of expensive wallpaper. His 3,000 shares broke the "market." His $96,000 investment shrank to $2,250—less commissions!

Incidentally, the SEC stopped the trading in that stock so other investors would not be hurt. Penny stocks have fantastic profit potential according to many people. The fast-buck artists believe this too. They are the people who make these profits, because they are the ones who sell to the gullible and greedy who dream of making a killing. In the past year or so, many stock brokers have begun to refuse to handle stocks that sell for less than $3. So who will sell your penny speculation for you?

WHEN TO SELL

Selling: the hardest investment decision is when to sell. I use several different factors to help me make this decision.

First I ask myself, "If I didn't own this stock, would I buy it at the current price?" If the answer is no, I immediately sell no matter what price I originally paid; the original buying price means little when you are trying to decide whether to sell. Do not fall into the trap of considering yourself locked into an investment because you do not want to pay the income taxes on a large profit. Pay taxes gladly and move on to another investment with more potential, and you will benefit more in the long run.

TAXES

Don't overstay your investment. When it has reached your desired profit level, get out and let the next investor carry on. Don't worry about losing some profit if it goes up more. If you couldn't find another investor who thinks your stock will appreciate more, then you would never be able to sell it.

Limit your losses but not your gains. Many investors will watch a stock holding sink lower and lower, waiting for it to recover so they can get out without a loss. Most of the time it will be a long wait. Smart money looks for potential investments that yield 10 percent as a minimum and hope for much more. They limit their losses by selling out at the first sign of weakness, and they hang on to the winners.

Selling your investments needs knowledge and you must not look back and have regrets. I believe in taking my profits and running, for the higher a stock goes the weaker are the investor's hands holding the stock. An exception is when a stock price rises into new high price levels; no one has a loss, so the only supply of shares will be from people who are selling to establish profits. In this case stocks seem to climb for good percentage gains before profit taking starts. There is a tremendous temptation to hang on until the last minute and try to squeeze the last possible dollar of profit out of an investment.

When you put in your order to sell, ask for a price just under a round figure. There may be 50 investors who have given the same order to sell at $50 to their brokers and you might miss selling out. Place your sell order at 49½ and you'll have a better opportunity of selling out near your desired price.

SOME STOCK MARKET TERMS

Capital gains: these are the profits realized when a stock is sold after being held 6 months by an investor. If you look at a stock price chart you can predict when some stocks, especially speculative or low-grade ones or those that have risen in price dramatically, are going to decline. For example, if a stock was purchased January 2nd at $10 per share, rose to $30 by February 1st, and stayed in the $30 to $35 range, you would probably find that about July 3rd to 6th the price would fall from $35 to $25 or less. This is due to an increase in the number of shares being offered for sale. The $10 investors, having qualified for the capital gains tax treatment, are now trying to sell in order to establish their paper profits.

Corporate take-overs and mergers may be for cash, or the investor may be offered stock in the surviving company. If you don't like the terms of a merger or take-over, you have the right to vote against it. If you don't like the surviving company you should sell out. Many times the swap of stock in a merger is on a tax-free basis and becomes very profitable for the investor. You should not end up holding on to a security that has no active market. These shares actually end up as a dead issue, and may not be worth much unless the surviving company offers to buy you out at a later date.

Letter stock is available for larger investors. It is stock that has not been registered with the SEC and is purchased with the understanding that it will be held as an investment and not redistributed. The shares are generally sold at about 60 to 70 percent of the current market price for the company's registered shares. The company usually promises to register the shares with the SEC when requested to do so by the stockholder. Letter stock is sold by the issuing company so it can secure money quickly, pay no commissions, and run no risk of depressing the existing price of its registered shares. This type of investing is recommended for well-heeled investors who are patient enough to wait for the larger profit potential. The restrictions on the sale of the unregistered shares are compensated by the low acquisition cost. Generally the minimum investment required is $25,000 or more.

Puts and calls: These are option contracts to trade stocks from 30 to 180 days in the future. A Call means you can buy 100 shares, and a Put means you can sell 100 shares of a named stock at a specified price and future date. The Call option is sold by the stock owner, who bets that the shares won't vary enough to make it profitable for you to exercise the option. Combinations of put and call options are called straddles, strips, or straps.

This is how they work: You buy a Call for $500 for 100 shares of "DDD" stock for 60 days at a price of $50 per share. If the market price rises to $100 per share you can exercise the option and buy the stock at $50 per share, or $5,000. You can then immediately resell the 100 shares for $100 × 100, or $10,000. Your profit would be the $10,000 minus the option cost of $500 and the share cost of $5,000, leaving a net of $4,500. If the stock falls below $50, you let the option lapse and lose your option premium of $500. If you own stock you can sell a call that would pay you the current market price if exercised. If the price falls you would retain the stock, and you have received the call premium as extra income. Puts work the same way, but on the sell side. About 85% of all puts and calls are allowed to lapse, so the option premiums are lost.

This type of stock market speculation is for extremely knowledgeable stock market traders. It is not recommended for new or small investors. You may secure further information from any New York Stock Exchange member or a Put & Call Dealer Association member.

Warrants: rights to purchase shares in a company at a specified level in the future. If a stock is selling at $10 a share and a warrant allows you to buy at $2 per share, then each warrant has an $8 leverage. If the stock rises to $20, the warrant has an $18 leverage. Thus the warrant moves faster (both up and down) than the underlying stock. This is why the profits on warrants can be extremely high. The investor's possible loss is limited to his warrant cost. Warrants may be issued with or without an expiration date. If the warrants have a time limitation they must be used in the specified period or they become worthless. Some warrant's time limits are as short as 5 days.

There are many new warrants on the stock market as a result of the numerous corporation mergers. Since the cost of issuing warrants is small and the warrant holders only have a right to pay the company more money for additional shares, many market professionals call them "funny money." For the speculator and market swingers, this is an excellent way to try for higher profits.

SHORT TERM TRADING

Uncle Sam makes money by getting the regular income tax on each profitable trade you make. The stock brokerage house and the registered representative make money by charging a commission each time you buy and sell, regardless of whether the trade is profitable or not. The short-term trader generally loses. One New York Exchange brokerage house surveyed 2,400 short-term trading accounts in 1967, a very profitable up market year, and found that only 18 percent of the traders made a profit!

When you hear traders telling about what a big killing they make in the market, remember they want to make themselves look good in your eyes, so they will "overlook" their losses or will discount the time cost element in their investments. Short-term trading is not a good idea unless you have market knowledge and a lot of money.

STOCK MARKET FADS

Many investors seem to be attracted to particular industries at the same time. Therefore, we have waves of popularity for the stocks of certain types of companies. In the late 1920's, all the radio set manufacturers were in demand. RCA was one of the hottest companies at that time. It took until 1963 for the RCA stock to equal its 1929 high! Many times, when one company stock does exceptionally well, stock brokers will push other stocks in the same industry. In 1969, the chicken franchises were good, along with nursing homes. In 1966, it was the color TV set makers, and in 1958, it was Florida land developers.

If fad stocks are being pushed up by stock fundamentals, such as increasing earnings or rapidly expanding markets, they can be good investments. The recent development of the performance mutual funds with their need for quick price appreciation has made the fund managers keenly aware of stock fads and how to take advantage of them. Mutual fund investment decisions attract large investment followings, and this in turn drives up the hot fad stocks.

The sure sign of a fad stock is a high price-earnings ratio for the entire industry. In the middle of 1969, the Dow Jones industrial PE ratio was 15 times earnings. Many of the hot hamburger and chicken issues at this time were cooking around a PE ratio of 70 times earnings! I advise you not to buy into an industry where the action is hot and the PE ratios are more than 30 times earnings. The smart money has already made the big profit and will sell at the first sign of fading popularity. If you get in early, ride it until the stock loses 10 percent of its high price and then sell. Don't ride a roller coaster. It isn't profitable.

THE NEW ISSUE MARKET

From early in 1967, the number of new companies raising money by selling stock to the public has increased to a tremendous flow. Many investors, or rather speculators, have bought stocks that have doubled and tripled within the same day. One new issue for a computer company tripled its first day, and when a call was placed to its home town, it wasn't even listed in the phone book! This new issue craze cannot last too much longer—sooner or later the bubble will burst and a lot of speculators will get hurt.

Most of the time new issues are priced by agreement with the underwriter and the issuing company. Generally, there is no earnings ratio, asset value, or other criterion used except what the market will pay. Many brokerage houses do not get enough new offering shares, so they will parcel them out to their best customers. This leaves the new or casual customer out in the cold. Of the 1968 new issues, about 1 out of 10 declined after they had been issued for six months or more. It is my estimate that most of these companies will go into bankruptcy, run through the capital raised and become dormant, just fade away, or be merged within the next 5 years. New company issues are recommended for speculators and gamblers.

New stock issues by established companies will furnish enough financial information in the prospectus so investors will be able to determine whether the investment suits their needs. If you invest in new issues, you must watch them very closely and sell when the price levels off for a few days, or you must plan for a long-term hold.

INVESTMENT ADVISORY LETTERS AND SERVICES

There are hundreds of investment advisors and stock brokers that publish reports giving stock market information or forecasts, business trends, and pure baloney. Many brokerage houses publish reports written by their analysts. Some of these publications are excellent, but most are worded in such a way that you can read into them whatever you want to read. The advice in others is so hedged with "iffy" statements as to be worthless. Many of the advisory market letters are compiled from other market letters and therefore contribute no new information.

Walston & Company, a New York Stock Exchange member, publishes a market letter that occasionally contains excellent information, and I have seen other financial information publishers adopt, re-use, or simply quote this information so that it spreads out like a ripple in a pond throughout financial circles. Many of these publications feed on each other, so their combined efforts sometimes cause stocks to react in the prophesied manner.

Market letters are helpful in calling investors' attention to market trends. Specific reports on individual stocks are probably the easiest and best way for investors to secure up-to-date information on stocks for possible investment. The financial advisory services that publish technical information such as economics, price and volume figures, price charts on individual stocks, etc. are useful if you know how to use them properly. Publicity releases should be treated with caution, as they furnish information from a biased viewpoint.

Many serious market investors hire investment managers to handle their accounts. If an investor does not like a mutual fund but wants to visit with a financial advisor and keep personal contact with his investments, he may find this type of service worthwhile. For the serious stock market investors there are numerous publications. Any stock broker will be glad to furnish you with all sorts of reading material. One of the better technical books is *Security Analysis* by Graham, Dodd, and Cottle. This book will give the technically minded investor a good introduction to stock market valuations and costs only $10.

If you wish to learn about the technical side of the market or become a professional stock market investor, I recommend that you write the New York Institute of Finance, 37 Wall Street, New York, New York, 10005, for information on their correspondence courses. Most of their courses cost about $100 each but are well worth it. They also distribute technical books. I also recommend that investors subscribe to *The Wall Street Journal, U. S. News and World Report*, and *Business Week*.

10

MUTUAL FUNDS

A Mutual Fund is a company that is organized to sell its shares and invest the money so received in securities or government obligations. Each shareholder participates in the ownership, voting, net income, and capital appreciation in proportion to the number of shares he owns. Mutual funds are registered under the Investment Company Act of 1940 and must conform to Securities & Exchange Commission rules and regulations.

As mutual funds are the fastest growing investment field and have many advantages for the average investor, this chapter will cover the background and technical points of funds, and Chapter 11 will give you pointers on how to select one or more for your personal financial plan.

At the end of December 1940, the year the Investment Company Act went into effect, there was $442 million invested in mutual funds. On December 31, 1970, the total investment by the public in funds was $52,000,000,000. This is growth by a factor of 120 in 30 years. It seems conservative to predict that within another 20 years most Americans will own mutual funds and this ownership will be as widespread as life insurance.

There are over 593 mutual funds being offered to investors today, with more going "public" each day. They vary from ultraconservative bond funds to highly speculative leveraged growth funds. The idea has been fostered by many stock brokers and insurance men that funds are for uninformed investors only. However, the Eaton & Howard Balanced Fund new account average is over $27,000. This record by a well-established mutual fund organization has proven that large investors buy funds. The fund industry's new accounts average over $4,000 each, which is a great deal of money for most people. When you consider that many funds will open an account with an initial investment of less than $100, you can readily see that many large accounts have been opened.

At the end of 1968, over 878,900 mutual fund accounts were held by fiduciaries or organizations. Fiduciaries such as banks, trustees, guardians, or administrators had over 744,700 accounts. There were 30,378 business corporations, 605 labor unions, 49,283 employee pension and profit-sharing plans, and 11,435 insurance or financial companies that owned accounts. There were 10,335 church or religious groups, 2,231 hospitals or orphanages, 7,921 fraternal, public, or welfare institutions that owned accounts. In addition, 2,159 schools and colleges had accounts, plus over 19,839 other institutional accounts that were not classified. This is a 14 to 1 increase since 1956, as there were only 61,494 of these accounts at that time. The large number of institutional accounts shows the soundness of mutual fund investing, since most of these could afford to hire their own financial advisors. The many benefits mutual funds offer institutional investors are exactly those enjoyed by the individual investor.

There is nothing a mutual fund can do for you that you can't do for yourself, IF you have the time, information, connections, education, and training in investing, and are wealthy enough to invest in many different securities to secure diversification. If 1,000 people invested $1,000 each in a money pool, they would have $1 million available to work with. This million-dollar capital makes them a wealthy investor. Then they are capable of hiring professional money advisors and diversifying. This is a simple explanation of what mutual fund investing is all about.

Most mutual funds have a minimum initial investment amount. Some, such as the Keystone group, have no limitations either for initial investment or for additions to an existing account. Other funds such as the Enterprise fund have an initial minimum of $50 and minimum additional investments of $50. The AMCAP fund has a minimum of $1,000 initially and $50 thereafter.

In many states there are contractual plans that require the investor to sign a contract to buy a certain amount of shares within a specified period. These contractual plans have come under fire or are banned in some states, such as California, as most of the total sales charge was taken out in the first year. Some of these plans take up to 50 percent of the first year's payments in commissions. Congress is now considering laws that will cut the initial sales cost to 20 percent of a particular payment and to not more than 16 percent of the invested amount in the first 4 years of the contractual plan. The investor must continue a contractual plan or he will find that he has paid a disproportionately high distribution cost. It is my recommendation that investors considering mutual funds use only voluntary plans and do not sign any sales contract that binds you to make payments for the next umpteen years.

In your consideration of a mutual fund, you may ask a mutual fund salesman, "What is the fund's yield?" or "What may I expect back when I finally cash in the investment?" You must remember that mutual funds are an equity investment and that neither the fund nor any salesman (registered representative) can make any promise that the fund will pay a certain yield. Nor can they guarantee that the investment will return at any time a certain number of dollars. Each fund has an available published record showing what its past performance has been. This may be used as a guide to see exactly how well it has performed. This performance must be judged against the investment objectives as stated in the prospectus of that particular fund. It is almost impossible to compare funds on a general basis as is done by some popular publications that put funds into arbitrary categories and then attempt to compare performances.

DISTRIBUTION CHARGES

One of the objections to investing in a mutual fund for many potential investors is the initial distribution charge. This charge generally ranges from 8.5 percent on investments of $10,000 or less to 1 percent on investments of $1 million or more. This initial sales charge is divided between the fund's underwriter, the selling broker, the salesman, bank and accounting charges, and taxes.

There are quite a few funds that are sold without any sales commissions or "load." These are generally operated by a brokerage house that buys and sells the shares in the portfolio. Their profit comes from the buying and selling commissions and the management fee. Many of the no-load funds have a redemption fee of 1 percent. Many brokers like myself do not handle no-load funds; like most other people, we have to earn money in order to live. When there is nothing in it for us, we won't sell it. It is a simple idea that some people don't understand. We get a few inquiries about no-load funds and always refer them to the particular fund's underwriter for information. If you want competent information, services, and advice, you must be prepared to pay a reasonable fee for them.

Many investors compare mutual fund distribution costs with stock commissions. This is like comparing the down payment on a leased car with the purchase price of one you will own. Investors must remember that a mutual fund account is a trust account that is constantly supervised and managed for him. The many mutual fund benefits illustrate this supervision and management.

Mutual funds' basic investing principles have been used for thousands of years, but the modern mutual fund development was begun in the early 1920's. The better organized and operated funds, and the most honest ones, survived the 1929 stock market crash and have prospered over the years. The statutory safeguards of the Investment Company Act of 1940 signaled the investing public's acceptance of mutual funds. Mutual fund growth is due to increased buying by investors and the reinvestment of dividends and capital gains by account holders. Also, the increase in the stock values of the funds' portfolios has contributed mightily to the growth of the mutual fund industry's $52 billion worth.

THREE BASIC PRINCIPLES

Mutual funds are probably the most convenient way for an investor to participate in the stock market or in an equity ownership. Through your ownership of mutual fund shares you are able to have the three most basic principles of investing working for you. These principles are time-tested and have proven to be profitable to follow.

(1) Diversification is essential; this means spreading your money over many different investments. In other words, you are not putting all your eggs in one basket. This principle was used hundreds of years ago by Chinese merchants who put their trade goods in several different ships. If one ship was lost in the Yangtze River rapids or stolen by pirates, the other ships might get through and their entire fortune might not be lost.

(2) Investment selection must be done carefully, with the proper research, study, and timing. The average investor is generally working and does not have the time to watch all of the developments of his investment.

(3) Professional supervision of investments is a necessity. Investing is a business that requires special training, experience in everything from stock market analysis to management. It takes still to make investing profitable. Good timing, both in buying and selling, is an art and is acquired by training; you must have the courage to make decisions.

OTHER FUND ADVANTAGES

In addition to having these principles working for you in a mutual fund, there are other advantages such as ease of purchase. Funds are sold by most stock brokers, and there are many sales organizations devoted entirely to mutual fund selling.

Redemption of fund shares is usually without charge, unlike

individual stocks on which you must pay selling commissions. The funds have to buy back any shares tendered them within 7 days, so there is always a ready cash market available.

Estate settlement in case of the investor's death is simplified, and mutual fund investments can be continued as most of them can comply with the prudent man rule. This is an investment guide that says investing by a fiduciary has to be what a prudent man would do under similar circumstances. To prevent fiduciary liability, many trustees and estate executors will sell all real property, stocks, and other equity investments and put the proceeds into debt securities like bonds or bank accounts.

Tax reporting is simplified, since funds furnish an annual report to each shareholder showing dividends and capital gains received during the previous tax year.

Accounting is simplified, as the investor receives confirmations showing each transaction during the year. Many funds have an annual summary sheet which is also sent to their shareholders.

There is no worrying about missed dividends, stock splits, or capital gain distributions. Also, warrants or conversion benefits will be taken care of automatically.

Custodian banks hold the fund's portfolio of securities in trust accounts. They pay for the fund's investments only when they have been delivered to the bank in proper or transferable form.

Funds are not taxed on their net income or realized capital gains if they pay out 90 percent or more of them to their shareholders. This "conduit" principle is a big advantage over investing in banks or insurance companies which are taxed on this type of income.

You have a wide range of choices when you invest in a fund. You may make a lump sum payment, have an accumulation plan and add regular small payments, reinvest both dividend and capital gains, or set up a withdrawal system so as to have a regular check to supplement your income. Most funds offer the investor the opportunity to reinvest his dividends and realized capital gains without sales charges.

Another benefit is that funds have a sales commission that

decreases with larger investments. Some funds allow smaller investors to accumulate their investments in order to qualify for a lower distribution charge.

All funds give annual reports and other financial information to their shareholders so they will know how the fund is performing.

TYPES OF FUNDS

The closed-end funds are investment companies that have sold a limited number of shares to investors. These shares are now traded like any other stocks. The trading prices depend upon supply and demand. If the shares are sold for more than the asset value they are at a premium, and if sold for less they are said to be at a discount.

Most mutual funds are open-end funds. That is, they keep creating new shares so they may be continuously offered to investors. They are sold at the net asset value plus a distribution charge. They are repurchased by the fund at the net asset value.

THE PROSPECTUS

This is an information booklet that gives all of the facts necessary for an investor to determine whether a particular mutual fund meets his investment needs.

A typical prospectus will start off by stating the general investment policy. From this you can determine whether the fund's objective, such as long-term capital growth, current income, etc., meets your investment objectives. Next comes a list of restrictions that cannot be changed unless approved by the fund's shareholders. Typically, total assets of the fund must be invested so that less than 5 percent will be in any one security, and it may not own more than 10 percent in any one class of securities of any one issuer. Stocks may not be bought for control of any company, nor may they be subjected to unlimited liability. The fund may not loan money, but the purchase of publicly distributed debt securities, such as bonds, shall not be deemed as the making of a loan.

The fund shall not purchase real estate, commodities, or commodity contracts, nor have margin accounts. The fund shall not engage in the underwriting of securities.

Among other common restrictions you may find some of the following: the fund shall borrow not more than 10 percent of its total assets; may not buy shares in other funds; shall not deal in puts, calls, or straddles; may not buy shares in companies in which officers or directors of the fund own more than 1 percent of the proposed investment; shall not buy shares in companies that sell tobacco, drugs, liquor, etc.

There will be a section on how shares may be purchased and on the distribution charges and the dealer re-allowance (commission). Next, there will be a section on special advantages such as letter of intent, which allows an investor to secure a smaller distribution charge if he buys a minimum amount of shares over a 13-month period. If the fund gives the right of accumulation this will be stated. This allows the investor to add all of his purchases so he may qualify for a lower distribution charge.

Then there will be a section that describes an open account plan, which allows the investor to add to the account as he sees fit. The reinvestment plan allows the investor to reinvest his dividend income or his capital gains (or both) at net asset value; or if there is a charge it will be so stated. A cash plan allows the investor to receive the dividend income or capital gains (or both) in cash. Many funds have a withdrawal plan that allows investors who have a minimum amount (generally $10,000) in the fund to receive a fixed sum at regular intervals.

How to redeem your shares is covered, and if there is any redemption cost it will be so stated. Most funds do not charge any redemption fee so there is no reason to buy a fund that has one.

The prospectus will describe how the net asset value of the fund is determined. This was changed by SEC rules on January 13, 1969. Now all funds value once a day, at the close of the New York Stock Exchange. The investor either buys or sells at a current net asset value which is determined by the fund's underwriter or custodian bank. The sales (ask) price is figured by adding the distribution charge on to the net asset (bid) price.

The income dividend and capital gain treatment will be described, including the tax qualifications the fund will comply with to secure a preferred tax treatment (the conduit principle).

The capital stock of the fund will be described. This section will generally cover voting rights and the number of shares authorized. Mutual funds are allowed to have only one class of shares, and all shareholders must have equal rights. Some states require that there be cumulative voting, which allows each shareholder to cast a number of votes that is equal to his shares multiplied by the number of directors to be elected. For example, if you have 100 shares and there are 7 directors, you would have 700 votes to cast for any number of directors, whether you gave them all to one or split them up between the candidates. This allows minority shareholders to elect a director to represent them on the board. I prefer to see cumulative voting privileges for additional shareholder protection.

The Custodian of the fund's securities will be named, and also the independent auditor who makes an annual check of the fund's books and actually counts the stock certificates and other assets of the fund. If there are any persons who own 5 percent or more of the fund's shares, they will be named. Also, the total number of shares and the percentage owned by the directors and officers of the fund will be shown.

There will be a section describing the management advisory contract. It will give the names, business backgrounds, and connections of the officers and directors of the fund. Each fund, under SEC rules, must have at least 40 percent of its directors independent of business connections with the fund. The management company and any cross-affiliations between the management, the underwriter, and the fund will be disclosed. It will cover the general terms of the advisors' contract and will discuss the management fee. A management contract must be favorably voted on annually by a majority of the independent directors or by a majority of the fund's shareholders. Management contracts may not be sold or transferred unless approved by the SEC and the fund's shareholders.

One section will describe how fund shares are sold, redeemed, and repurchased. It will describe any special arrangements or contracts for sales or financial advice with other financial companies. Commissions paid to the management company and the underwriter will be shown. This will generally be followed by a section describing the underwriter (distributor) of the fund's shares. The terms of this contract will be disclosed, plus any dealer re-allowance if the shares are sold to the public through other broker-dealers.

There will be several financial statements. Among these may be a historical highlight of the performance of one share of the fund. A per share income and capital change schedule will show expenses that will equal or exceed any dividend income, as the fund will be concentrating on capital gains. In this type of fund the net income is purely incidental. In an income fund the expense ratio should be less than 4/10ths of 1 percent or it is too high. There may be a "mountain" chart that shows how an investment of $10,000 (a required figure by the SEC) has done over the life of the fund or for the past 15 years. There will be a portfolio list that shows each security, the number of shares, the market value, and its percentage of the total net asset value. If it is a diversified fund the various industry categories and their percentage of the total net assets of the fund will be shown.

Sometimes funds will show the cost of each investment. Since the purchase date is not shown, the investor cannot judge whether the investment was a good one, because the only criterion for this is the difference between cost and market value. Many times these figures show a loss, but the investor must remember that all performance figures for funds include all of the losers and mistakes! Incidentally, funds are allowed to conceal under miscellaneous investments up to 5 percent of the fund's total assets. This enables the management to conceal any current buying or selling. Many investors, if they knew what stocks a fund was trading, would rush into the stock market and thus disturb the market price before the fund was able to complete its proposed acquisition or sale of stock.

There will be a statement of assets and liabilities and a statement of income and expense. This shows you how much the management company was paid for its advisory services. There will be the auditor's statements on paid in surplus and his verification letter.

Many mutual funds now include in the prospectus an application form and a letter of intent form. All salesmen are required to deliver a prospectus to possible investors before or during the sales presentation. If you make an investment, you must be allowed to keep a prospectus.

THE LIFE INSURANCE AND MUTUAL FUND PACKAGE

Any study of economics shows that there are recurring cycles of prosperity and depression. As a hedge against both of these possibilities, one modern method of financial planning combines the protection of life insurance with the flexibility of mutual funds.

Life insurance is very vulnerable to inflation, except as pointed out in Chapter 5. A certain "profit" can be made if the insured dies in the early years of any life insurance policy. When thought of in this manner, life insurance is also a hedge against inflation. Over any longer period of time, however, mutual funds will build up more capital than the same amount invested in cash value life insurance.

These modern financial packages work on four different approaches:

(1) *Mutual funds and term insurance.* This plan operates by the purchase of term insurance to provide the investor with the time necessary for his mutual fund investments to complete the desired equity build-up. Most of the time, decreasing term insurance is used since it is expected that as the investor gets older the insurance need will decrease. As an illustration of this type of

plan: In 1944, a 40-year-old man with $1,800 per year available made a purchase of a $25,000 reducing term life insurance policy at a cost of $350 annually. The balance of $1,450 was invested in the Investment Company of America (ICA) for the period from 1944 to 1968 (25 years). In the first year, death benefit was $25,000 plus the $1,350 investment, or $51,350. At age 65, there was no insurance left but the mutual fund had a total value of $80,612 assuming all dividends and capital gains were reinvested.

(2) *Mutual funds plus a cash value (ordinary) life insurance policy.* This split fund package gives a higher number of fixed dollars than plan (1). It also enables the investor to convert his mutual fund holdings into the insurance policy to provide guaranteed retirement benefits at present annuity values. For an illustration of this type: In 1944, a male age 40 with $1,800 available yearly used a 50–50 split between funds and insurance. This buys $40,000 of ordinary life and leaves $900 to be invested in the ICA mutual fund (use period of 1944–68 for illustration). The first year death benefit was $40,000 plus $900 accumulated investment, or a total of $40,900. At age 65, death benefit was $40,000 plus accumulated investment of $49,960, or a total of $89,960.

(3) *Mutual funds and financed life insurance.* These plans are more suitable for higher tax bracket investors, as the out-of-pocket insurance costs are mainly interest and are deductible for tax purposes. As interest costs rise each year, the investor hopes that the mutual fund side will increase its dividends to absorb them. The life insurance policy loan rises each year, and this is supposed to be offset by increased value in fund shares from additional new purchases and an increase in the net asset value of the accumulated shares. It is impossible to show an exact history that has any meaning, as interest costs have risen to abnormally high levels and past history is so distorted as to be relatively meaningless. The use of mutual fund past performance figures are just a guide, as there is no assurance that they will be repeated.

(4) *Equity funding.* The idea is similar to number (3), but all of the available money is invested in mutual fund shares. Then the fund shares are used as collateral for a loan to pay the insurance premium. This has the added advantage that each

invested dollar works twice: once when it is deposited for fund shares, and again when borrowed to pay the life insurance premium. Generally, ordinary life insurance is used so there will be policy cash values. If the investor lives, the policy cash value can be used to pay a major part of the loan against the fund shares. The investor builds the mutual fund account by purchasing fund shares each year. This, plus any increase in the net asset value of the fund shares, should cover the margin requirements of the increasing loan. On September 1, 1969, the Federal Reserve Board established for the first time a 60 percent margin on equity funding plans. This means that a lender can finance $40 of insurance premiums for each $100 in mutual fund shares owned by the investor.

This is the most speculative plan and will probably show a greater return over a longer period of time (a minimum of 10 years) than the other plans. Its weakness is that if the stock market declines and the total value of the mutual funds shares goes down too much, the investor may be obligated to put up additional money or fund shares to raise the collateral level to 60 percent.

Of the four combinations of insurance and funds, I prefer the term-insurance-plus-fund approach because it does not involve borrowing. The increasing loan gives me an uneasy feeling when I consider that I must continuously borrow and pay an ever-increasing loan and current interest charges. I would prefer to own my insurance and funds outright and be able to stop the plan at any time without complications or an immediate cash problem. In the event that shares must be liquidated, there could be a large income tax payment due on the appreciated value of the funds sold to pay any loan.

The generalizations made in this chapter and the next must not be considered the final word on funds. There are many additional questions that should be answered before you invest in a fund.

Most investors want to compare funds to find out which one is the "best." The simple answer is, "The fund that comes closest to fulfilling your investment needs." The best way to find this fund is to ask any investment dealer. I am sure he will furnish you with all the literature you need or are willing to wade through to make your selection.

There are many excellent books and publications available about funds, but individual prospectuses are the finest information available. I recommend that you secure a copy of the Weisenberger *Investment Companies* and read the first 100 pages very carefully. It has more good, factual information than you can find in any other publication. You may find one at your library, or you can get one from the Nuveen Company, 61 Broadway, New York, New York 10006. If you know a stock broker I am sure he will be glad to let you read his copy.

11

HOW TO BUY MUTUAL FUNDS

The last chapter discussed the technical side of mutual funds. This chapter covers what to look for when you are considering buying a fund.

I would like to point out that I am biased: I consider mutual funds the best all-around investment medium available today. I make my living selling mutual funds, and most of my company's income is from mutual fund sales. Therefore, I *do* have an ax to grind! If I did not believe mutual funds were the most outstanding investment opportunity existing today, I would not be in the business of mutual fund investing.

There are now over 500 different mutual funds being offered to the investing public. They have a wide range of investment objectives and management policies, and the profit opportunities depend primarily upon the degree of risk the fund managers are willing to take. The establishment of a fund account means that the investor must choose between the many funds oriented towards his investment objectives.

CLASSIFICATION OF FUNDS

The following is an arbitrary classification of funds so you will have a general base from which to compare investment objectives and past results. Each mutual fund's prospectus will state its investment objectives and its type. To illustrate each of the classifications listed in this chapter, I will quote from the prospectus of a fund that was selected at random, and from a wide choice. *Funds used as illustrations in this chapter are not recommended as the investment choice in the particular classification.* To select a fund for your investment needs you should consult a trained mutual fund salesman or stock broker.

INCOME FUNDS

The Channing Income Fund's "primary objective is to pay current dividends to shareowners with due regard for the need to protect capital values. Growth of income and capital is an important secondary consideration." Further, their prospectus states that bonds and preferred stocks tend to be used where high current income and stability of capital is desired. Common stocks are normally acquired for their growth potential as well as their dividends. These statements classify the fund as a conservative investment suitable for older investors who want income and enough growth to keep up with inflation.

As a sub-classification, we could place bond mutual funds in the income group. While rising inflation has caused a loss of principal over the past ten years, the income produced has been in the 5 to 6 percent range. However, since they have shown little safety of buying power or conservation of the investor's principal I find that I cannot recommend them to my clients. The investment objective of the Keystone B-1 is "to secure the relative price stability of the high-grade bond class with as liberal a yield as can be obtained." This fund invests in high-grade bonds for a higher degree of stability.

BALANCED FUNDS

These are organized for investors who wish to pursue a moderate course of investing as shown in the following example. The Channing Balanced Fund's objectives are "conservative long-term growth of both capital and income, reasonable current income, and preservation of capital to a degree consistent with prudent investing." The prospectus further states that "in the selection of all investments the emphasis is at all times on financially strong, promising companies regarded as leaders in their respective fields."

Also, common stocks will never exceed 75 percent of the Fund's assets. Balanced funds will spread their investment portfolio to include bonds, common stocks, preferred stocks, debentures, and cash or cash equities. This diversification of investments is governed by the fund's articles of incorporation or by decision of the Board of Directors. The balanced funds do not rise or fall as much as growth or stock funds do in the stock market cycles. The income dividends tend to be more stable over the years. The Eaton & Howard Balanced Fund invests mainly in New York Stock Exchange listed securities for income and stability. This is a high-grade fund. Other balanced funds may try for more income or more growth, but still emphasize stability.

GROWTH FUNDS

Most funds can be classified as growth funds. The Winfield Growth Fund states, "The potential for capital growth will generally be the only basis for the selection of portfolio securities, and any income received from such securities will be entirely incidental." What separates these funds from the more speculative ones is the following statement, also from Winfield: "The Fund's normal expectation in purchasing a security is that its anticipated performance level will be reached over the longer rather than the shorter term."

Growth Funds: Performance of the Go-Go Varieties. The Putnam Growth Fund had a growth rate of 91 percent for the year 1959. This outstanding performance led to more speculative investing and the Go-Go funds. These growth funds take greater chances by investing in smaller, perhaps unknown companies, and will also take short-term profits. By 1967 the fund industry was pushing "performance." Investors were being sold funds for long-term investing based on performance recorded in a few months or years! In 1968 about 70 percent of all new fund investments were being made in performance funds. The main criterion that distinguishes a Go-Go fund from a growth fund is that it will borrow money to use a leverage for additional investing. The new funds now stress good investment fundamentals.

Illustrating the Go-Go funds is the following, from the Explorer Fund's prospectus: "The Fund's investment objective is maximum long-term growth of capital. It will seek this goal by investing primarily in securities of relatively small, unseasoned, or embryonic companies." It further states that it is for investors with substantial resources. Minimum initial investment is $25,000, with additional investments of $500 minimum. The WinCap Fund is a new performance fund that has "the sole objective of capital appreciation. Immediate income return is incidental to growth of capital in the selection of investments by the Fund." The Fund's present portfolio consists primarily of speculative securities. The management intends to invest in securities with potential for capital appreciation, regardless of whether the issuers are new or well-established companies. Annual portfolio turnover rate will exceed 100 percent. Fund borrowing may not exceed 25 percent of its new assets.

These two funds illustrate the variety of performance funds available. WinCap is suitable for persons who know something about investing, are willing to absorb a loss if one should occur, and are patient enough to ride out any down market. The Explorer Fund is suitable for the larger, sophisticated investors.

Growth Funds: the hedge variety. Another type of fund has been developed to secure more performance than regular growth or performance funds. These funds are attempting to use the more sophisticated techniques of the stock market. The Tower Fund, Incorporated, "is a fully managed, non-diversified, leveraged hedge fund whose primary objective is capital appreciation rather than receipt of current income from portfolio securities. The Fund is not intended as a complete investment program. It may supplement customary investment practices by at times employing speculative techniques which may entail greater than average risks. The Fund may borrow sums to purchase securities, use short sales, purchase and sell put and call options written by others, engage in short-term trading, purchase and sell warrants, and may invest in special situations." The portfolio turnover is expected to be over 100 percent annually.

This fund is a good illustration of the new type of fund that has come on the market in the last two years and that caters to the speculator. These funds do not have any track record at this time, so they cannot be judged by comparison with growth funds' past performances. It remains to be seen whether advance investment techniques, such as short selling, will enable hedge funds to outperform growth performance funds. Hedge funds must assume more investment risks to achieve more performance results. If they can outperform other funds, they will merit the investor's confidence and his financial support. These funds are recommended for the more affluent investors who want capital gains and are willing to assume more risks to get them.

Specialty Funds: non-diversified or industry funds. Funds that concentrate their investment activities in one or perhaps two industries have had varying degrees of popularity over the years. When life insurance stocks were hot in 1961 and 1962, the life insurance funds had outstanding growth records. Since the years 1963–67 were rough on life stocks, these funds have fallen out of favor with investors. Many of these funds have renamed themselves and have diversified their investment portfolios. The Life Insurance Stock Fund changed its name to the Life Stock and Growth Fund, and instead of being 100 percent invested in life insurance companies now promises to invest at least 40 percent in life insurance companies and at least 40 percent in other industries. The Century Shares Trust prospectus states that their principal objective is to "enable investors to acquire a security of moderate prices which will represent a diversified, managed investment in the common stocks of insurance companies and banks." The ratio of expenses to average net assets is among the lowest and in 1968 was 0.46 percent. Portfolio turnover is around 8 percent. This would be further classified, in my opinion, as a conservative fund.

In order to satisfy the changing ideas of investors, fund managers keep bringing out new types of funds. One new type of industry fund, for example, invests in certain technological fields such as oceanography.

The Ocean Technology Fund's "primary investment objective is growth of capital through investment in common stocks and other securities having common stock characteristics, primarily those issued by the technological and service-oriented companies in the field of ocean technology." Under "Investment Policies" the prospectus continues: "The Fund intends to invest at least 60 percent of its investment portfolio in companies principally engaged in the ocean technology field." It expects that its annual rate of portfolio turnover will be between 50 and 70 percent. Also, the Fund proposes to borrow money to invest only when the net assets are equal to at least 300 percent of the borrowings. This is a performance fund in a non-diversified technical field. This type of fund should appeal to technically minded investors who are connected with the oceanographic field and are willing to invest their money in the area of their normal interests.

NEW FUNDS

A great many new mutual funds have been formed in the past few years, and they are being created at a faster rate each year. When a fund is small, it is easier to establish a growth record. The fund's advisors are able to buy small amounts of shares in new, small, developing situations or regional companies. Many times, new funds are formed and held off the public market for a year or so. This enables the fund to establish a performance record which is sometimes spectacular. This system was used by the Putnum Growth Fund, the Fairfield Fund, the WinCap Fund, and others. Performance records thus established are not really fair, nor can they be used to describe a fund's past record since the entire investment philosophy has later been changed.

The change from a limited amount of money to a constant flow of additional money is a major one. It is better to invest in new funds which are being offered by established mutual fund organizations. Established management companies have an existing sales organization, experienced personnel, sufficient finances to pay operating expenses that may exceed the new fund's limited money, and contacts to keep them up to date on investment opportunities. These new funds are created by management advisors who find that their existing funds have grown too large and can no longer sustain a constant growth pattern. Some of the newer funds started by existing management advisors are the Dreyfus Leverage Fund and the WinCap Fund.

Besides the new oil drilling funds described in Chapter 12, some real estate funds have recently been started. They invest in mortgages and real estate interim financing paper. (See Chapter 6 for fuller details.)

CLOSED-END FUNDS

These investment companies do not offer their shares continuously or redeem them. The shares are traded like any other stocks and are bought and sold through stock brokers. You must pay a commission for both buying and selling. The shares are priced according to supply and demand. If you pay more than the net asset value they are said to be at a premium, and if less they are at a discount.

Another variety of closed-end funds is the DUOFUNDS. These seven funds were started about January, 1965. They have two different classes of shares. The income shares receive all of the income dividends on both classes and have a minimum guaranteed dividend that rises during the life of the income shares. After a limited period, usually 18 years, the income shares are either redeemed in cash or exchanged for capital shares. The capital shares receive no dividends but get all the capital gains on both stock classes. This should improve the performance record of the growth shares.

Over their short history, I have noticed that the funds have been able to invest in some very high income-producing securities which are more than sufficient to produce the required dividends. This enables the fund managers to be more aggressive and invest in more non-income-producing issues for possible larger capital gains. It is cheaper to buy shares in these funds, as the regular mutual fund distribution charge is larger than ordinary stock commissions. However, if you pay a premium for these shares, you must count the premium as part of your cost. If you do not hold the shares until the conversion period or sell them back to the fund, you must count on paying another commission when you sell them.

The puchase of any duofund shares calls for proper timing and a careful comparison of performance records, premium price, and commissions with a regular mutual fund. This is a recommended investment for long-term holding for conservative investors.

SIZE OF MUTUAL FUNDS

The size of a fund has a very important influence on investment performance. The larger funds become unwieldly and move in a pattern that is close to popular stock market averages such as the Standard and Poor index. Extremely large funds such as the Wellington Fund or Massachusetts Investors Mutual have a big problem finding and buying or selling large blocks (hundreds of thousands) of shares. Since their investment portfolios are over $2 billion each they must invest a minimum of several million in each stock issue or they would have the bookkeeping problem of handling hundreds or thousands of different issues.

The large block requirement forces these large funds to invest in the large, stable, older corporations that have large amounts of issued stock. These corporations have usually reached the fully developed stage and are very stable with smaller growth patterns. Investing in extremely large funds is recommended for older investors who are content simply to have their investments doing better than in a bank or savings and loan account. These funds' stability will vary along with the general prosperity of our country as measured by stock index averages.

In 1967, 22 large mutual funds with assets over $300 million each had an average 43.6 percent net asset gain. Sixty smaller funds with assets under $300 million showed a 62.5 percent growth rate. All of these funds were classified as maximum capital gain funds. The specialized mutual funds, such as life insurance and bank funds, had a loss of 0.6 percent. This illustrates the weakness of an industry fund when that industry is out of favor with investors. In 1969, 19 growth funds with over $250 million each had an average loss of 14.0 percent compared with the Dow Jones loss of 15.19 percent.

MARKET REACTIONS

Most funds have records that can be favorably compared with the Dow Jones index over long periods of time. Performance figures for funds include all mistakes, losing investments, and down periods in the stock market. Most fund managers pray for a drop in the stock market every few years so they can buy good stocks at low or reasonable prices.

Funds cannot establish a performance record in a stock market decline such as that experienced in 1969 and 1970. How can any financial advisor say "Look at my record—I lost only X percent, which is better than the Y percent that the stock market is off"? Fund performances are made in rising stock markets and by out-performing comparable funds or the Dow Jones averages. The Dow Jones averages were off 15.2 percent in 1969. Out of 388 mutual funds only 18 showed a gain. The best was the Templeton Growth Fund, up 19.3 percent. The average 1969 mutual fund loss was 14.33 percent compared with the Dow Jones loss of 15.19 percent. Some of the more highly publicized funds and salesmen's favorites sustained the biggest losses. The Enterprise Fund, which was up 116.3 percent in 1967, lost 20.3 percent in this down period. Combined, the Enterprise record shows a large profit for the longer-term investor.

As institutional buying is now a major influence on the stock market, it is obvious that these large investors can and will cause the stock market to fluctuate. In the 1969–70 market decline the heavy selling of blue chip stocks by banks was a major contribution to poor stock market performance and deepened the drop in the market value of many individual stocks.

PORTFOLIO TURNOVER

This is the rate at which the investments owned by a fund are traded. This figure is shown in the prospectus. The higher this percentage, the more the fund will stress growth and capital gains. The average for most funds is about 45 percent, while some speculative funds will trade 150 percent or more. In my opinion, unlimited trading is one of the most important tools a fund manager can use to get performance. Some of the problems created by a high turnover are higher brokerage commissions, short-term trading profits, high fund fluctuations, and large capital gain payouts.

INVESTMENT POLICY CHANGES

Many times they do not show up in the performance records or fund charts, yet policy changes affect a fund's entire investment philosophy. Life insurance stocks did very poorly, and in 1968 many were selling at around 60 percent of their 1962 market value highs. The Life Insurance Fund did not keep up with the averages or even with other funds. The fund was renamed the Life and Growth Stock Fund on February 1, 1968. The investment policy was changed from 100 percent investment in life insurance companies to a minimum of 40 percent. At least 40 percent must now be invested in other industries. The evaluation of this fund must be made on its record since the date of the investment policy change. The earlier record has no bearing on today's performance, and the investor should consider this a new fund as of the investment change date.

CHANGES IN MANAGEMENT

Here is a hidden factor in the evaluation of a fund's performance. The investor must know the background of a fund and not merely depend upon a chart or performance record. In the fall of

1962, the Vanderbilt Mutual Fund changed management advisors. A slightly heavier emphasis was placed on growth, and the fund's growth rate since then has been outstanding. At the same time, the new management was more aggressive and sales-conscious and improved the sales organization. The new management company had more financial reserves and strengthened the entire operation. The fund is now among the top twenty-five in growth and income. Similar changes have done wonders for other funds such as the Winfield Fund and the Enterprise Fund. The Nesbitt Fund, which was renamed the Dreyfus Fund, has compiled since 1951 one of the most outstanding records in the investment industry, under new management.

INVESTMENT DECISIONS BY MANAGEMENT

Until recent years, funds were operated by investment advisory committees. At committee meetings, suggestions and supporting data were presented by analysts as a guide to committee action on proposed investments. When mutual funds began to stress growth performance—meaning a fast rise in market price—many funds turned the operation of investment decisions over to individual managers. These managers were allowed to make their own decisions and act upon them promptly. I believe the Shareholders Management Company was the first to divide a large fund into several sections and place individual managers in competition with each other. This type of operation proved to be very successful. In 1967, the Enterprise Fund's net asset value per share rose 116.3 percent, which made them Number One for the year.

Many performance funds do not have the fixed management fee of 0.5 percent that was common with the older funds. They now often have fees that vary from 0.2 percent to as much as 4.0 percent of the fund's annual net asset value. The higher fees are paid when the fund out-performs some index such as the Standard and Poor or Dow Jones stock market averages. This incentive spurs the management companies to show positive results so they can profit as the fund's investors profit.

DECEPTIVE GAINS BY USE OF LETTER STOCK

"Letter stock" is a stock issue that has not been registered with the SEC. This type of stock carries the same privileges as any other, but it is not freely tradeable and can be sold only in SEC-exempt or private transactions. The issuing companies usually guarantee letter stock buyers that they will register the shares at a later date. As it takes about 6 months and many thousands of dollars to register a stock issue, many times new or expanding companies issue letter stock in order to raise money quickly.

Because the stock has trading restrictions and the shares should be held for at least 2 years, letter stock is usually sold at a discount. Many speculative funds buy these discounted shares and immediately value them on their books at the market price of similar registered shares. By upvaluing stocks bought at a discount, these funds immediately increase their net value per share, a practice that gives them a nice percentage increase and makes them look good in charts and competitive fund performance ratings. The more letter stock a fund has, the less liquidity needed for its redemption obligations.

In June, 1968, the no-load Mates Fund suspended share sales and redemptions until it could revalue downward the upvalued shares of an investment in Omega Industries. When the fund was downvalued, the net asset per share was almost cut in half. As this was a no-load fund not sold by most mutual fund salesmen, many investors could not keep up with the developments. Investors should examine fund prospectuses carefully and determine what their investment policy is on letter stock. Small amounts in growing companies can provide excellent profits, but large amounts can cause trouble for the investor and possible losses.

WITHDRAWAL OR REGULAR INCOME PLANS

Most mutual funds have a withdrawal plan that allows investors to receive a check on a regular basis. Each fund establishes certain minimum amounts such as $5,000 or $10,000 to open an account, and the withdrawal checks must be at least $50 or more. This is one of the most convenient ways for investors to establish a regular income. Withdrawal plans are growing in popularity as widows and retired people learn of their advantages.

One of the best records in the growth funds shows that if you had invested $25,000 in the Oppenheimer Fund on April 30, 1959, and had taken out 8 percent annually, or $166.67 per month, you would have had $67,908 left in your account on December 31, 1968! If in the same time period you had taken a monthly check of $250 (12 percent), you would have had $41,605 left. Such a record shows why withdrawal plans are becoming so popular. The total number of withdrawal plans in 1960 was 24,000; by 1969 there were 278,000. The Investment Company Institute estimated that by the end of 1968 there was $5.0 billion invested in these plans, and investors were receiving checks totaling over $17 million a month.

DIVIDENDS AND CAPITAL GAINS

Most funds will reinvest dividends and capital gains without sales charges. In 1950, income dividends amounted to $111,540,000, and in 1969 they were up to $1,181,693, of which $688,000,000 was reinvested. This shows investor confidence and satisfaction.

SALES OF FUND SHARES

The Board of Directors of the fund executes a contract with an exclusive distributor (underwriter) for the sale of the fund's shares. The underwriter contracts with stock brokers and mutual fund sales organizations to do the actual retail selling to investors. The broker employs registered representatives (salesmen) to contact the investing public. When an investor agrees to buy shares he signs an account application and makes a check out to the fund's agent. All stock brokers receive the same commission from the funds, and all commissions charged are equal.

Many times investors receive more personalized attention from a small brokerage house than they would from a large stock exchange member brokerage house, which generally caters to larger investors. The small independent broker may have more mutual fund knowledge, since that is his specialty. Many funds have their own captive sales organizations which sell only their own funds, such as the Investors Diversified organization. Upon receipt of the application, the fund opens an account in the investor's name and sends him a stock certificate or a confirmation (receipt form) showing his investment record. I usually recommend that investors use the confirmation receipts and not have stock certificates issued. If the investor loses a stock certificate, it is difficult and expensive to get it replaced with a new certificate.

FUND SALESMEN

There are many excellent qualified fund salesmen who can give you sound investment advice and put you into the fund that fits your financial needs. However, there are a lot of salesmen who do not know the business; although they have passed the necessary examinations and have been licensed, they are not competent. Salesmen cannot and should not guarantee you anything but an opportunity to invest in American enterprise. If a salesman guarantees you a specified yield, income dividend, or growth rate, or claims that you cannot lose part of your investment, you should not buy from him. You should check with his employer or another broker, or ask him for his personal guarantee in writing (then watch him back off). Past fund history can be used as a possible indication of what you might hope for in a fund's future, but these records are not guaranteed.

As in any other investment, the more you know, the better you can judge what a fund may do for you. Be sure to pick a stock brokerage house that handles all types of funds and is not a captive organization for a single group. An independent securities dealer can be a tremendous help in selecting the proper fund or funds for your investment program.

I recommend mutual funds for most investors. You may discover that you need more than one fund; no single mutual fund can be all things to all people.

12

MISCELLANEOUS INVESTMENTS

Most people have a natural instinct to accumulate, collect, or hoard, and it can be very educational (and sometimes amusing) to read a hobby magazine and see just what collectors are willing to buy.

An investment in art objects, antiques, beer labels, circus posters, ashtrays, barbed wire, books, pulp magazines, cars, fire engines, sea shells, bottles, or other articles is classified as a collector item.

COLLECTOR ITEMS

In our present expanding economy, it seems reasonable to assume that the amount of money spent on collector items will increase and that the prices of such items will rise. There are no available statistics on the present gross sales of businesses that cater to collectors, such as antique stores, hobby shops, coin and stamp dealers, etc. Lower-priced items such as stamps, coins, bottles, and buttons generally have a profit margin of 100 percent or more per item, but the businesses depend on a large volume of small sales. Higher-priced items (for instance, a Van Gogh painting) have a unique appeal and are often in such limited supply that a large profit or loss can be made on each sale.

Your profit potential depends upon the number of sales you

make each year. If your investment capital can be used to buy and sell 5 times a year, you have a turnover of 500 percent. Even if each item involves a low profit, you may show a handsome over-all profit if you have a large gross volume.

This investment field requires comprehensive knowledge of the item, of trends in collecting, of sources of additional items and the resale market. When you locate an item to buy, you must assume that the seller is also knowledgeable. While bargains may occasionally be found, there are lots of bad "buys" around to trap the unknowing buyer. A friend of mine purchased, at a reputable auction, an "as is" Chippendale chair. While restoring it, he removed some paint—which he found was covering a Sears Roebuck label. The value of his "bargain" went from $175 to zero because he could not differentiate between a reproduction and an original.

If you intend to make money by selling collector items, you must consider your travel costs and the time spent in looking or buying as additional investments. Don't write off your time as a hobby or a pleasure trip. It is easy to fall into the trap of mixing pleasure with business and to lose money. You must be able to divorce yourself from your items, and not hoard them or become attached to them. You must sell them! You cannot be a sentimental collector and a businessman at the same time.

The biggest problem in making money in collector items is finding continuing, adequate sources of supply. For example, many antiques are one-of-a-kind, so you must handle many different items such as glass, furniture, and silver in order to be able to reinvest in more items when you sell your current stock.

Most collectors buy at retail, sell at or below wholesale, and never have any profit. A collector item businessman selling to the retail buyers generally does most of the work, but he also gets the largest share of any profits. You must have enough capital to buy in quantity or pick up collections at wholesale and to carry your investment items in inventory until you are able to resell them at a profit. Your capital requirements are extremely varied and may range from a few cents to tens of thousands of dollars per item. Over-all capital required may be only $25 or so for a few items or thousands of dollars for a comprehensive stock.

If you resell at wholesale you will cut your expenses, but you will lose part of your potential profits in fees or commissions to an auction house, a salesman, or a retailer who sells your material. If you wish to sell at retail, you must set up facilities to deal with the public and incur the ordinary business expenses of rent, labor, taxes, insurance, overhead, and advertising. Much of the ordinary business overhead can be kept to a minimum, since you can store the items in a garage or in any spare space in your home or office. Items such as furs, paintings, or other valuables may require cold storage or a bank vault for safekeeping, thus increasing your overhead. Your biggest expense will be in the labor of cataloging, storing, sorting, repairing, and otherwise handling your items for resale. It is difficult to find qualified skilled labor, and wages rise every year.

Many collector item investors find that they have unintentionally gotten into a full-time business as they try to do the necessary work themselves. Collections of average or poor-grade material have low resale value—junk is junk. Labor is expensive, and it may cost more to sort or catalog a collection than the collection is worth.

Investing on your own behalf generally doesn't require any licenses, but it may if you develop it into a business. It is wise to check with local government agencies to be sure. Subject to a specific ruling by the Federal Internal Revenue Department, most collector item profits are taxable as a capital gain if held for over 6 months.

Your best sources of additional information are your local libraries, investors in similar items, or any of the specialty publications devoted to your item. There are literally hundreds of clubs and societies organized to promote interest in specific collector items; visit your local bottle society or railroad fan club.

A SAMPLE COLLECTOR ITEM: STAMPS

Stamp collecting is the world's most popular hobby, but few collectors realize a profit or even break even on the money invested in their collections. This is because they buy retail and sell at or below wholesale. They buy for sentiment, enjoyment, and interest, not resale potential. If you want to recover most of your money or show a profit, you must observe a few basic rules.

Always collect stamps in the best possible condition: clean, nicely centered with borders, with light cancellations, and not torn or otherwise impaired. Do not invest in precancels, revenues, first-day covers, or plate number blocks, as these items have a very limited resale market due to lack of general interest. Always but a complete set including the high values. Buy the scarcer stamps first or when you can find them, for most collections are made up of cheap material cataloged at just pennies each (you can buy world-wide collections of 20,000 different stamps for $75) and you cannot resell them profitably. You can buy good collections of cheaper material at from 5 to 10 percent of catalog price. Specialized collections of rare, valuable, or unusual material may show a large profit if you can find a buyer. Always add collateral material to a specialized collection including stamps on cover and cancellations. You should collect popular countries such as the United States, Germany, Switzerland, Sweden, Spain, Australia, the Vatican, etc.

Avoid stamps from the communist countries; they issue too many stamps each year. Many African and Arab countries issue stamps for the sole purpose of extracting money from collectors, and this wallpaper does not rise in value. Some of the French and English colonies also issue unnecessary stamps, which dims collector interest. Topical collections such as space issues or those in honor of men like Churchill or President Kennedy lose much of their value when the public loses its interest. Topical collections on sports and Boy Scouts retain high public interest; they have shown nice advances in catalog prices and will continue to do so.

Avoid investing in stamps from Central and South America. There are many worthless fakes and counterfeits which are difficult to detect. There is also a general lack of collector interest.

Knowledge and current information are essential in this field. I suggest you subscribe to either *Linn's Weekly*, P.O. Box 29, Sidney, Ohio 45365, or to *Western Stamp Collector*, Albany,

Oregon 97321. It is helpful to join a national society such as the American Philatelic Society, P.O. Box 800, State College, Pennsylvania 16801. Also, talk to a local stamp dealer who is an American Stamp Dealers Association member.

COINS

Much of what has been said about stamps also applies to coins. You must be knowledgeable and you must invest in quality. Always buy the scarcest coin in each set, as this key coin is the one in demand and changes a sentimental accumulation into a worthwhile collection. It is best to specialize in larger-sized silver coins or gold coins of popular countries such as the United States, Germany, Mexico, or Austria. Remember that people in the industrial or advanced nations have the money to buy and the time to enjoy a hobby. The emerging nations are struggling to survive and have little time or money for hobbies.

Many people have invested in bags of quarters, halves, and silver dollars from the U.S. Mint at face value. Today, coin stores and speculators are offering to sell bags of "rare" coins at prices way above face value. These are the investors who will profit the most. While coin collecting is a growing hobby, there are too many hundreds of thousands of silver coins that will come on the market if prices increase. Also, silver coin bag speculators will become increasingly restive if prices do not move up, and they will sell regardless of the current market. This overhead supply will limit future profits.

The U.S. Treasury has removed from circulation most of our silver coins and these are being melted down for their silver content. This will decrease the number of coins available, but it will be 10 years or more before collectors can determine what coins are really in short supply. Coin values depend upon supply and demand. In 1960, 1903–0 silver dollars sold for $1,200 each. In 1965, when investors began buying the sacks of silver stored in the Federal Reserve Banks, hundreds of thousands of rare coins turned up, including the 1903–0's. As a consequence, in 1967 you could buy one for $15, and the current market in 1970 is $32.

In June, 1969, the U.S. Treasury department removed the ban on the melting of U.S. coins for their silver content. This added about 800 million ounces of silver to our industrial supplies. It would be difficult for an investor to buy silver coins on the open market, pay the smelting charges, sell the silver bullion, and make a profit. Over a longer period an investor would do well to buy silver bars and hold them in place of coins.

I have used coins and stamps as examples because they are the most representative collector items. High public interest, a supply of inexpensive items, and enough rare items to excite the wealthy collector have made them popular. But judging by past performance, neither coins nor stamps are as profitable as common stocks, real estate, or savings accounts.

The real major profit in collector items is the making of new friendships that can last a lifetime. This, plus the pride of ownership, should be the reward found in collecting.

CONCLUSIONS ON COLLECTOR ITEMS

Collector items are not a suitable investment for most people. It is very easy to become attached to the items through sentiment or pride of ownership, and then you become unwilling to sell. Most resales are made to specialized markets, so you may not find a ready market at the time you wish to sell.

For retired persons who wish to supplement their incomes and do not have to consider the time expended as an expense, collector item investing can be profitable and very rewarding. It will enable them to supplement their incomes, develop new interests, and keep busy. Many hobbies depend upon part-time retired people as a main source of supplies, information, and know-how. Collect for your enjoyment first. Resale or profit should be only a minor consideration.

OIL SPECULATION

Investing in an oil well or a drilling fund is for the speculator or the swinger. It is usually done to secure a tax shelter or in hopes of making a "killing." Under current income tax laws, $225 22.5 percent) of each $1,000 of oil production income, up to percent of net income, is tax-free. Other mineral deposits have 5 to 23 percent tax-free depreciation allowances. These natural resource depletion deductions can be taken as long as the investor receives income from the natural resource, even though he has recovered his entire investment in depreciation.

Another oil venture tax advantage is the intangible drilling deduction, which is the cost of drilling the well. This is a deductible expense, and not a capital investment which would be depreciated over the life of the investment.

Salvageable assets such as buildings, casings, pumps, pipe, and tanks are depreciated over the productive life of the well.

A majority of oil wells are failures due to a dry hole, insufficient gas pressure, too much water, too heavy an oil, or some other problem. If the well is abandoned for any reason, the investor can take the investment as a tax loss to balance out his regular ordinary income. To the investor in a 50 percent income tax bracket, it means that the government is taking half the risk. The investor can carry losses back 3 years or carry them forward 5 years. A few years ago one of my friends bought a ⅛th interest in a Texas development well. The well was drilled in 11 days and abandoned when no oil was found! While this was unusually fast, it shows what can happen.

Many investors buy a fractional share (¼th, ⅛th, etc.) in one well and take a chance. In my opinion it makes more investing sense to purchase an oil participation program, spreading the risk and owning a share in a bigger venture.

OIL FUNDS

Since early 1968, a large number of oil drilling programs have been started. These are commonly called oil participation programs or funds. These funds are run by a management company, more often than not the operating oil company, for a set management fee plus a share in the net income. The oil company pays for the field expenses, overhead, and taxes out of the total revenue.

All income from the wells drilled in the participation program is pooled, and after paying expenses the net income is split between the operating company and the investors. Generally the split is on a 50–50 basis. A few companies split 75 percent for the investor and retain 25 percent. They do not participate in oil income returns until the investor has received his entire investment back. These particular programs are better for the investor, as he receives a more generous share than in most other participation programs.

Oil participation funds vary greatly in expenses, details, and operations. The following points will enable you to make a reasonable judgment on which fund would suit your financial needs, the risk involved, and its fairness to all concerned:

(1) Do the promoters (the oil company) have an extensive and successful background in oil field operations?

(2) Will the drilling program be based upon sound geological information verified by an independent geologist?

(3) What is the initial sales charge for buying a participating interest in the drilling fund? (It should be 9 percent or less—most funds charge 6 to 9 percent.)

(4) Are the promoters buying any participation interests in the fund? If so, this is a big plus factor. They are betting their money along with yours.

(5) Are your investment units or participation ownership held in partnership or tenants in common? Partnership means that you could be held liable for any unpaid bills or incurred liability. I suggest that you check on the liability risk with your attorney and invest only in a venture that sells its participation units as tenants in common or limited partnerships.

(6) How much is being raised for the drilling fund? It should be over $4 million and less than $25 million. Most oil companies cannot effectively utilize more money, as the number of drilling prospects is limited. If an oil company has excess money there is a great temptation to drill more wells on marginal information and take a bigger risk than usual.

(7) Does the fund have a balanced drilling program? For a more profitable fund, the available money should be budgeted to

spend perhaps 25 percent on exploratory wells (wildcats) and 35 percent on development wells. The balance of the program should be used to drill production wells. There are exploratory drilling programs that drill wildcat wells only, but it must be realized that these are highly speculative and are a go-for-broke type of investment.

(8) Do the investors receive 100 percent of their investment back before the oil company participates in the oil revenues?

(9) Will your investment be returned to you within 4 years? If not, the venture will not prove very profitable. You must consider the interest that could have been earned on your money in the same period of time.

(10) Do the oil company's costs, expense estimates, and management fees compare favorably with other companies in the same business?

Various state corporation commissioners, the drilling fund managements, and others realize the speculative nature of drilling ventures. To protect small investors from losing their life savings, usually there are minimum investor requirements. A few of the commoner requirements are: minimum net worth of $50,000; a 50 percent or higher income tax bracket; minimum investment of $5,000; investment experience or knowledge.

I recommend investing in oil if you meet the foregoing minimum requirements. Also, if you are a professional man or business owner with a large steady income, you may find it worth your while to investigate a drilling program. All oil investors must be able to accept a complete investment loss without becoming emotionally disturbed. As many of the oil investment advantages are based on income tax allowances and depreciation schedules, investors should realize that oil investment profits depend upon Congress. Any changes in the income tax laws cutting depreciation allowances will eventually devaluate the investment and cause a capital loss.

25% exploratory (wildcats)
35% on development wells.
40% to drill production wells.

13

KEEPING WHAT YOU HAVE

All of us are faced with a problem that we like to sweep under the rug or push off into the distant future. *It is hard to save money.* This is the primary problem. We have discussed savings and how to plan to save. We have discussed how to invest. Now let's cover the subject of keeping what we have saved, earned, or acquired.

The best way to save money and keep it is to follow a budget. The problem is, most people who do budget seem to leave out the most important payment of all—the payment to your savings or investment accounts. Most people say they will save whatever is left at the end of the month. I found that with me there was too much month left at the end of the money!

My present budget is set up on the following basis: a payment of 10 percent of my take-home earnings into a mutual fund investment; 5 percent to my spendable savings account, then a payment for the next car. The balance is divided between the necessities (house payment, insurance, gas, lights, water, food, and household expenses) and personal expenses (dining out, travel, shows, entertaining). Lastly, I make speculative investments with any remainder.

To many, the installment buying of expensive durable items

such as a car, furniture, or jewelry means a form of savings. This is actually spending; the item will not increase in value over the years. Everything you buy on an installment plan also costs you from 5¢ to 25¢ per dollar more. This means you either buy that much less or have to earn that much more. If you control your installment spending you will give yourself an automatic tax-free pay raise! This savings could be the 10 percent that I recommend you save each month. What you don't pay in installment charges, interest, and fees will amount to a tidy sum when saved and invested.

So let's not fall for the lure of the advertising huckster: "You can afford it . . . it's only a dollar down and a dollar a week!" It's up to you to change this line to your benefit. Say "I can save and invest it . . . for it's a dollar down for me and a dollar a week for my accumulation of wealth!"

I believe there are only two things you should buy on the installment plan: your home and your investments.

The way to financial failure is to spend your money in the following order: necessities, recreation, waste, and yourself (investments). If you want to guarantee success you should spend your money first for yourself (investments), then necessities, recreation, and waste.

Businessmen are allowed to take a depreciation deduction each year for the wearing out of equipment and for obsolescence. You and I are getting older, we are slowing down and tiring. We must replace our income, and part of all you earn should be yours to keep. Why work all your life for someone else? Unless you keep part of what you earn you have been nothing but a dollar slave or servant all your life.

INTEREST COSTS AND INSTALLMENT BUYING

The biggest pocketbook leak for everyone is interest costs. When we are young or first married, we want and need material goods such as a house, furniture, and car. Every once in a while we give a fleeting thought to preparing for the time when we will come to the end of the income road. From the age of 20 through the 50's, our earnings rise until the last pay check; then it's retirement pay. For most people the problem is not how to make more but how to save some.

The best way is to keep part of what you earn and make it work for you. The extra price you pay for goods bought on the installment plan is a price cut you can make very quickly, although it is not easy to change buying habits.

Most national credit cards are the gateway to easy buying. "Just charge it on a revolving plan and pay a little each month." Cards such as the BankAmericard charge you a minimum of 1.5 percent per month (18 percent per year). Since most people pay when billed, the interest charged is for part of a month, and when calculated on an annual basis the actual interest rate can be 20 percent or more. Most stockbrokers will tell you that if you make 15 to 25 percent per year on your investments you have done extremely well. So why pay for the use of a credit card the same amount that you find hard to earn?

There are several rules to observe in credit buying that will keep money in your pocket:

(1) Use credit as a convenience and pay the account off before you are charged interest.

(2) Use credit accounts that do not charge interest.

(3) Do not buy non-durable items on credit. This means pay cash for clothes, trips, etc.

Remember that if you use credit, an item that is priced at $99.99 could cost you $115 very easily. Is it worth the extra $15?

ESTABLISH A SPENDING "SAVINGS" ACCOUNT

Open an account at your bank, a savings and loan, or a credit union, and use it strictly for spending on larger items. Make a payment to yourself each month, feeling that this account is for spending and not savings. When you want to buy an expensive item such as a car, furniture, or a trip, you will have the money available. Instead of making payments to a finance company you'll make the payments to your spending savings account and save the interest charges.

To rebuild the account after a big purchase, make a monthly payment, the same you would have made if you had used credit. It may mean putting off buying something now to establish the account. If your present car is paid for, start making a monthly payment to your spending savings account. Or drive your present car at least one year after you have finished making the payments, put the same amount into your account, and watch it grow. When you go to buy the big-ticket item, you'll be pleasantly surprised to find how much you can save by paying cash. To sum it up, you'll profit four ways: (1) earn interest; (2) save paying a high rate of interest; (3) cut the purchase price in many instances; and (4) save on both income and sales taxes.

COLLATERALIZED LOANS

Here's another way to save on interest charges. If you go to a bank to borrow money and can put up stock certificates, mutual fund shares, real estate, or other assets as collateral, you will be able to borrow money at a simple interest rate. This method of borrowing can cut interest costs in half. Check with your banker and find out just what you can save. It will be profitable for you.

FINANCE COMPANIES

Many people borrow money from finance companies. Statistics show that many people who file individual bankruptcy owe money to finance companies. Their interest rate on small loans is about 2.5 percent per month, or a simple interest rate of 30 percent per year. The rate charged for loans over $700 is generally the state law limit, or 1 percent per month. You can see that it will cost you $12 per year more to borrow $100 from them than to borrow from a bank. The only time you should borrow from a finance company is in a desperate emergency when you have no other place to turn for cash. Easy credit will get you into a real financial bind, and the extremely high interest cost makes it very difficult to pay off this type of loan.

LIABILITY INSURANCE

These policies are relatively cheap and are sold by most insurance agents. They offer the policyholder a method of protecting his lifetime savings and investments from law suits. It seems that there are a lot of suit-happy people who feel that money derived from a law suit is easy money, and they are able to hire attorneys who feel the same way. Many investors have liability insurance on their cars, and some have it included in their homeowner's general insurance policy.

As the cost is low, I recommend that you purchase a liability insurance policy with limits of $100,000 per person and $300,000 per accident. With a policy this size you will find that the insurance company will assist you with legal advice or even supply an attorney if you are unfortunate enough to be sued. Your ownership of property is sufficient to establish the fact that you have invited others to come onto your property. If they are hurt and it can be proved you were negligent, you will pay.

HOMESTEAD LAWS

The old adage that a man's home is his castle has produced in many states a remarkable law. Homestead Laws are designed to protect your home against legal claims which would become a lein on your property. Your creditors can secure a court order to sell your home to raise money to pay the lein. If you incur debts, adverse lawsuit decisions, or a business failure, or even if your teenager has a traffic accident which requires you to pay damages, your home equity is protected up to $20,000 (in California). If your equity in your home is over $20,000 and the house is sold, you would retain $20,000 to use to buy a new home within a 6-month period. All you have to do is file a declaration of homestead with the proper public official, usually the county clerk. Homestead forms are available at most office supply or stationery stores. It is a very simple one-page form. For expert service and peace of mind, you may find it worthwhile to consult an attorney.

GIFT-GIVING

Here's one way you may keep your assets in your family and save on taxes. Each taxpayer has a lifetime gift tax exemption of $30,000. There is also an additional $3,000 annual gift tax exclusion, or $6,000 if your wife joins in making it a joint gift. Most gift-givers cut inheritance taxes by giving gifts to their wives and children.

At the present time Congress is holding hearings that may affect gift tax laws and schedules. Each Federal Internal Revenue office and State Inheritance Tax Board has current tax information free for the asking. Additional information may be secured from public or tax accountants, your attorney, your banker, or a financial advisor. To qualify something as a gift the donor must not have any right or power to get the gift back. There are gift tax forms which you may secure from the Federal Internal Revenue Service whether the gift is taxable or not. Filing this form will establish the gift and prevent it from being challenged at a later date by the IRS.

TRUSTS

A trust is a legal arrangement whereby property is held by a trustee under certain specified conditions. Trusts can be set up during one's lifetime or under the terms of a will. There are two ways to set up a trust. The revocable declaration of trust form allows the maker of the trust to cancel or revoke the trust at any time and have the trust's assets returned to him. The irrevocable trust form is used when the trust's assets have been given away to the trustee for supervision under the conditions of the trust for the named beneficiaries. In the irrevocable trust the maker has given away the assets, even though he may be the trustee, and therefore he does not have the use or benefits of the trust for himself, but only for his beneficiaries.

Revocable living trusts offer several benefits. The assets upon your death are automatically transferred to your beneficiary at the moment of death. As they do not become part of your estate, these assets are not subject to the claims of your creditors. You can revoke the trust at any time prior to your death and the assets will revert to you. You can name yourself as trustee, which is used mainly when a trust is set up for personal dependents such as parents, wife, or children. Since you are transferring assets to yourself and can reclaim them, you incur no tax liability. Your named beneficiary need not be consulted before you take any action regarding the trust such as cancelling it, changing the beneficiary, or adding others.

In the event that your named beneficiary dies before you, or becomes incapacitated, or fights with you, you do not have to worry about making any changes in the trust. Owning property in joint tenancy puts a burden on the survivor to prove that he really owns a part of the property, or the entire property may be assessed for inheritance taxes. The creation of a trust avoids the open court publicity that attracts confidence people and enables them to select unwary and inexperienced investors as their victims. Trusts will distribute their assets to your beneficiaries as you have designated, and your decision cannot be readily challenged by greedy or jealous relatives.

As trusts are not part of your estate, your beneficiaries are saved the cost of estate probation and can make substantial savings which may run as high as 10 percent of the trust. It eliminates attorney's fees, court costs, probate and executor's fees on the trust's assets.

Revocable trusts are included in computing the value of an estate for federal estate tax purposes. Irrevocable trusts are exempt from inheritance taxes, as the assets were given away before death.

A trust establishes an investment that can be retained by your beneficiary. As estate executors are personally liable for mistakes of judgment or for fraud, they have a tendency to sell any stocks, property, real estate, and bonds and invest the estate's assets in government bonds or bank savings accounts. At the close of probate, many beneficiaries are handed large sums of cash. Many are not capable of investing this cash properly and therefore stand a good chance of being cheated or making poor investments so their inheritance will be lost.

Many widows are left in comfortable circumstances and within a few years have lost everything. If you don't believe this statement, stop reading right now. Ask your wife, son, daughter, or any of your beneficiaries this question: "If I gave you $50,000, what would you do with it if I weren't here to advise you?" Take your time, wait for an answer, and don't let it turn into a joke. Some answers will be, "I'd ask our minister, attorney, next-door neighbor, your brother, a salesman in real estate, a stock broker or insurance office, the bank." Now that you know how little (in most cases) they know about investing, don't you think you should plan right now for their financial future and protect them from themselves?

Trusts are very flexible and many different provisions can be used to solve different financial problems. You can provide income directly to a dependent without incurring income taxes. You may set up a limited (10-year) trust with all income going to a dependent, such as a parent, wife, or child, and at the end of the trust the principal will revert to you. Since your dependent will probably be in a lower income tax bracket you can save on income taxes.

Trusts can be set up to serve more than one generation. You could give your wife or anyone else the right to receive the trust's income and provide that upon her death the trust's assets would go to the successor beneficiaries such as your children. In this manner your wife would have a lifetime income, pay no inheritance tax, and upon her death the capital would go to your children who then would be liable for any taxes due at that time.

A popular trust version is one in which a trust is set up in the wife's name with the husband as beneficiary. The husband will make payments to the trust, and as he can give up to $3,000 per year to his wife without incurring gift taxes, he can build up her personal estate. Usually the husband dies first and as the wife will have her own resources she will not have to pay any inheritance taxes on her trust; it is her personal property. If the family should need money for some emergency, the wife could withdraw money or terminate the trust within a few days without difficulty. This type of trust can save thousands of dollars in the right situation. My investments in mutual funds are set up in trust for my wife, and she has investments in trust for the family. For further information, I recommend that you read the book *How to Avoid Probate* by Dacy. Everyone who is seriously concerned about keeping what he has accumulated should read this book.

The larger your estate, the more you need a trust that is written for your specific financial needs. A trust when set up to solve your problems can work wonders. I recommend that you consult an attorney before creating any trust. However, one word of warning: many attorneys do not like trusts and will do their best to prevent you from setting one up, as they will lose executor fees, attorney's fees, court appearance time, filing fees, etc. So find an attorney who is sympathetic to trusts. Many mutual funds have simple trust forms that are good for small uncomplicated estates or for setting up education trusts for children.

INTEREST DEDUCTION

Many people have investments that have reached the point of showing a large profit, and they do not want to sell because of the amount of money they would lose in taxes. The following describes a method of tax saving that has worked for many.

If a man has a $100,000 investment, now worth $200,000, he would pay a large capital gains tax if he sold it. If he gave the investment to his son he would have to pay a gift tax. So the father sells the investment to the son for $200,000, the fair market value, at a rate of $10,000 per year over 20 years, plus a minimum interest rate of 4 percent per year. The father would pay capital gains taxes on only $5,000 each year, since the other $5,000 is a tax-free return of his capital. The father will also pay income tax on the interest received. The father's tax bracket should be smaller than the son's tax rate, so there should be a tax savings. The son would have an interest deduction of $8,000 the first year (decreasing each year) to offset his regular income, thus cutting his income tax. At the end of 20 years, the son will have an investment that cost him $200,000 and that should have risen in value. This increase in value has been accomplished on a tax-free basis. When the son sells he will have to pay capital gains tax on any profit. This is one way to furnish financial support to family members at a minimum cost to the rest of the family. It will also allow a father to pass on his business to his family without the necessity of securing outside money by taking loans or selling an interest.

TAX SHELTERS

One of the most popular financial pastimes today is beating the government out of taxes. Not counting lawbreakers, most investors who try to avoid taxes use the game called tax sheltering.

Tax sheltering is the postponement of taxes by use of tax loopholes. It includes using deductions for property depreciation, natural resource depletion (oil), interest payments, gifts, charity deductions, multiple corporations, etc. Sooner or later the investor must accept the fact that either he or his heirs will have to pay the deferred taxes.

The major advantage in tax postponements is that the investor has the opportunity to use the postponed tax dollars for other investments. These investments must stress capital growth or the entire operation will be worthless. Regardless of the anticipated tax saving, all investments must be able to stand on their own. Tax-sheltered benefits must be considered only a part of the investment picture. Many "tax shelters" are poor investments that have been dressed up by tax gimmickry. For maximum tax advantages, the smart investor will consult with tax experts who will specifically design a tax shelter program to fit his personal financial needs. This is definitely not an area of investing where the go-it-alone investor can prosper.

The main investment weakness in tax shelters is that they are dependent upon the federal income tax laws, which can be changed very drastically. It is evident that Congress some time in the near future will plug some tax loopholes. Then investors will find that some tax-sheltered investments will lose their tax advantages, which in turn will cause a capital loss. Tax shelters are especially beneficial to people who pay 35 percent or more in income taxes each year or who have investments with large profits. Persons with lower incomes will find that to secure many of the advantages of tax sheltering he will incur heavy costs that are out of line with the amount he has to invest. Also, the small investor may end up with all his available resources tied up in one investment.

WILLS

Every adult should have a will. If you haven't had one written up the law of succession will, through court proceedings, write one for your estate. Most of us would like to have our worldly goods go to the people we select. Many people think you should be sick to make a will, but the best time to make a will is right now while you have the chance.

Unfortunately, we all know families that have been broken by fights over an estate. It seems that love, family ties, honor, and decency disappear when beneficiaries get greedy over inheritances. So help your survivors when you depart this life—have an attorney create a set of asset disposing instructions that will comply with your wishes and existing laws. It is my belief that the small fee an attorney charges to draw up a will is probably the cheapest fee you'll ever pay for such an important document. If you don't have any material goods, it is still advisable to have a will. Will forms can be purchased for a dollar or so at most office supply or stationery stores. Probating an estate without a will takes about 20 months longer and costs many more dollars than if a will governs the estate.

For further information, consult an attorney. If you do not have one or know where to ask, call your local bar association. The local office of the Internal Revenue Service or State Inheritance Tax Board will furnish you with tax information.

AFTERWORD

It is becoming much easier for you to be a millionaire. The Federal Reserve Bank estimated that there were 40,000 millionaires in 1958. By 1974, there were 160,000!

To show you how easy it is for you to become a millionaire, take the sum of $10,000 for a starter and compound it at the rate of 15 percent per year. That will make you a millionaire in 33 years.

The time to start work on that initial $10,000 is right now, while you're young. As one ages, one begins to experience certain fears. The older the person, the more basic the fear.

The fears of old men are not very pleasant: they fear cold and hunger, sickness and neglect, loneliness and oblivion.

Your dreams do not have to include these fears, especially if you follow some of the basics I've set forth in this book. Your dreams can be quite positive, in fact, *because one good investment is worth a lifetime of labor*.

If you invest well today, you are beginning to fulfill the dreams of happiness you had yesterday, and you're starting the foundation for tomorrow.

Invest today.

INDEX

75 10 9 8 7 6 5 4